*Little Things
Remembered*

Little Things Remembered

A Cuban Immigrant's Family Ties

Stories by

Maria Luisa Salcines

PUBLISHING

AUSTIN, TEXAS

LITTLE THINGS REMEMBERED:
A CUBAN IMMIGRANT'S FAMILY TIES
BY MARIA LUISA SALCINES

Cover Art: Jorge Salcines
Cover Photo: J. Carlos Diaz
Cover Graphics: Michael Qualben

PUBLISHED BY
LangMarc Publishing
P.O. Box 90488
Austin, Texas 78709-0488
1-800-864-1648

Library of Congress Control Number: 2004108766
ISBN: 1-880292-750 $12.95

DEDICATION

This book is dedicated to my parents, my husband, and my children, in this order because this is how they came into my life.

Mami,
Your grace, wisdom, love and faith in God have guided me through life. I learned to be a mother and a wife watching you care for our family. For all that you are and all that you have given me. *Eres muy querida, Mima.*

Papi,
Your love for my mother and your commitment towards our family, and the courage you have always shown when facing life makes me proud to be your daughter. Thank you for all the sacrifices you have made for us. *Te quiero mucho.*

Jorge,
My love, you have always believed in me. You have fulfilled all my dreams and more. For the love and happiness, and the passion you bring to my life. You have my heart and life, forever. *Te amo.*

To my children: Jorge, Carlos, and Maelia
Nothing I will ever do can compare to the joy I felt the day I became your mother.
My life would mean nothing without you. Always remember that faith and family are the most important things in life. *Los quiero mucho.*

TABLE OF CONTENTS

SECTION I
LEARNING FROM LIFE

SECTION II
A MOTHER'S LOVE

SECTION III
LESSONS IN LOVE

SECTION IV
THE CUBAN IN ME

ACKNOWLEDGEMENTS

I have been very fortunate to have people in my life who have supported and encouraged me through the years. I want to thank my brother, Lazaro, my sister-in-law, Griselle, and my nieces whose love and support mean a lot to me.

My cousin, Maelia, sister of my heart, and my best friend, I could not get through life without you. We have shared a lifetime of laughter and tears. I look forward to growing old together and watching our children grow.

Carmen and Juan, you were my friends many years before you became my in-laws. Thank you for raising such a wonderful son.

A special thanks to *The Monitor* newspaper and all the wonderful editors I have worked with through the years. Thank you for allowing me to share my stories with the Rio Grande Valley.

My sincere appreciation is reserved for Kathryn Kvols and the International Network for Children and Families. May our RCB family continue to grow so that all children can be raised in a loving home.

And last but not least to all the administrators, teachers, counselors, and parents I have worked with throughout the Rio Grande Valley. Your commitment to children and families is making a difference.

INTRODUCTION

Each and every one of us has a shiny star in our life. But sometimes we spend so much of our time looking over our shoulder at what others have that we don't take the time to see how bright our star really is.

Life has no smooth roads for any of us, but we aren't always aware of it. We meet a celebrity or drive past a mansion and wonder what it would be like to be that person or to live in that house.

When we focus on our dreams and stop worrying about what others have, we can learn to appreciate the extras life brings our way. I believe that the less we ask for, the more that life gives us.

When I was a little girl, I never realized how little I had. I did not realize how poor we were and what a struggle life was for my parents those first few years in the United States. My parents were always happy. I never heard them complain or talk about things they wanted.

I was taught to be happy for others and to enjoy beautiful things, even if they were not my own. As I got older and my parent's financial situation improved, we continued to be the same. We moved into a larger home and we were able to afford nicer things, but we continued to be the same people inside.

My heart is and will always be the same as it was when I came to this country as a Cuban immigrant. The day I lose that will be the day I forget the most precious and most important lesson my parents have passed on to me.

Cubans know that what is important in life has little to do with what we possess because from one day to another, all we have can be taken away from us.

What defines a person has nothing to do with his surroundings or his possessions, but everything to do with who he knows he is, what he dreams he can do, and the love he has in his heart.

SECTION I

LEARNING FROM LIFE

HAVING FAITH

Faith is a gift. It is a light we carry in our hearts that does not always shine brightly, but can never be put out.

Faith is something we must have in order to survive life on this earth. It doesn't matter what religion your faith is. Its presence in our life and the outcome of the knowledge we gain from it has a deep effect on us as human beings.

Faith doesn't just happen! We're not born with it. It's something we have to learn from our parents. Our parents light the candle and keep it burning for us while we are children.

Eventually, we learn how to keep the candle lit, and as we get older we learn how to protect the flame. Faith is a string that binds generations together. It is something we learn from being near people who have faith. It's highly contagious, and once it finds itself in you, it fills your heart with peace.

In my room we have a frame with a picture of the Sacred Heart. The metal frame used to be bright gold, but now it's dull and even chipped in some places. The picture is a bit yellow around the edges, and it has faded in some spots.

I don't remember exactly when it was my mother framed the picture. It must have been a few months after we came from Cuba back in 1963. My mother had been looking through a magazine when she saw the beautiful picture. The next time she went down town, she stopped at McCrory's on Main Street and bought the least expensive and only frame she could afford.

The image of the Sacred Heart blessed my parents' home for years. It wasn't until my mother bought a crucifix and hung it over the entrance of our home that the frame became mine.

When I got married, the first thing I packed in my suitcase was the Sacred Heart frame. It has been with me for years, blessing my home as it did my parents' home. The image of the Sacred Heart is a symbol of my mother's faith, and with it I learned about having faith.

Every time I look at the picture, it reminds me of my parents and all they have been through as Cuban immigrants. I believe that even though we all pray differently, we are all praying to the same God. Our faith links earth and heaven, and through our prayers God hears our messages.

God doesn't always answer our prayers the way we would like. Faith is not in what we can fully understand, but in what we don't know and yet believe with all our hearts.

Thomas Blake said it best when he wrote:

"Every morning lean thine arms awhile upon the window sill of heaven and gaze upon thy Lord, then, with the vision in thy heart, turn strong to meet thy day."[1]

A Teacher's Touch

When I was in elementary school, I felt isolated from everyone, and it was hard for me to make friends. Only someone born in another country can understand how different things are in the United States.

Parent Teacher Associations, Girl Scouts, football games—none of these things existed in Cuba. My family and I spent the first few years adjusting to our new home and learning new customs.

In 1969, while I was attending Victor Fields Elementary School, one very special lady influenced me and helped bring me out of my shell. I remember Mrs. Della Croce Meyers as a very sweet woman who was always kind and patient.

With her loving way, she invaded my little world and became a special part of my life. She tutored me whenever I needed help. She met my parents and even invited me to her home. She made me feel very special about being an immigrant.

One day Mrs. Della Croce asked if I would like to speak about Cuba at a luncheon given by the Pan American Round Table. I was ten years old and terrified, but I loved my teacher and if she thought I could do it, I couldn't let her down.

The luncheon was held at the Texas Hotel in Pharr. I don't remember the details, except that I got up in front of a room full of people and told them about the day my family and I left Cuba. I ended the program by playing the piano.

I have never forgotten that day and how important I felt. It helped me gain self esteem, and I believe it was a turning point in my life.

Mrs. Della Croce left Victor Fields, and my family moved to the Milam School District. I was in sixth grade and nervous about changing schools. My first day in Milam turned out to be one of the happiest days I've ever had. When I walked into my new classroom, Mrs. Della Croce greeted me with open arms.

Teachers have a huge responsibility. They hold a key to a very important part of a child's development. Over the years as a mother and a PTA volunteer, I have seen wonderful teachers who have encouraged and supported their students. I have also met teachers who shouldn't be teaching.

I have heard coaches calling their players "losers" and then expecting a winning team. It is discouraging to see a professional act this way.

Attitudes are acquired throughout life from significant others: parents, extended family, teachers, friends, national figures, even performers. One negative teacher can change your child's attitude towards school, toward life—just as one wonderful teacher can inspire and bring out the best in your child.

We all have the ability to make our dreams come true. It doesn't matter how old a child is or what his past history has been or what his present circumstances are. He can do anything in the world he wants as long as he believes in himself.

Every child is unique and every child has unfulfilled dreams and capabilities. We should never allow anyone to take those dreams away from us.

YOUNG AT HEART, YOUNG IN SPIRIT

"It is not by the gray of the hair that one knows the age of the heart." Bulwer-Lytton

The pattern of aging is very much like the rising and setting of the sun and the moon. Aging is like the progression of the stars and the turning of the seasons, which are part of nature's pattern. It is part of God's plan. It makes us slow down a bit and wise up to the fact that we have to stop and enjoy life.

One of the things I admire most about the American culture is that regardless of how old you are, life is enjoyed to the fullest. In the Spanish culture, growing old means giving up certain activities. Although many Spanish grandparents have modernized their views, many still adhere to the old ways.

For example, my grandmother wouldn't wear certain colors because she found them inappropriate for a woman her age. After a certain age, she never again wore a bathing suit.

Retiring in America is a beginning, not an end, to a way of life. It means having the time to travel and learn new hobbies. It's making new friends and having time to create joy in life.

Pick up the latest issue of *Maturity* and you'll find articles on computers and articles written for spirited individuals who are always on the go. Senior citizens in this country ride bicycles, play golf and tennis until they are physically unable to do so. When that happens, they find something else to do.

A few years ago while on vacation in Colorado, my husband and I met a group of senior citizens who were touring the country on Harley Davidson motorcycles. The youngest in the group was in his early sixties. After we admired their motorcycles, we watched them drive off towards the Rocky Mountain National Park.

Age has nothing to do with a person's capability to enjoy life. If anything, age is like a permission slip written by nature that allows you to do whatever you've always wanted. The older you get, the more you realize life is fragile, and you have to enjoy it.

During the winter months in the Rio Grande Valley, Winter Texans make this area their home. Simplicity seems to be the way of our winter friends. The majority of them live in mobile homes; they've gotten rid of their excess baggage. It must be exhilarating to just be able to pick up and go.

These spirited individuals not only come to have fun, they also spend a lot of their time volunteering and sharing their talents with the community. It makes so much sense to live, to learn, and then to teach and share the knowledge with others.

As the winter months approach, I begin to see our winter friends more and more in the grocery store and in our restaurants. They're teaching me how to grow old gracefully.

My parents and my in-laws are modern Cuban grandparents whose suitcases are always packed and ready to go. They have incorporated in their very tradi-tional Cuban lifestyle the wonderful American way of aging.

Someday when it's my turn, I hope I don't shock my children when they see me and my "*viejito*" driving out of town on a Harley motorcycle. Like George Bernard Shaw, I also think, "Life is not a 'brief candle.' It is a splendid torch that I want to make burn as brightly as possible before handing on to future generations."

Seize Life! Make it Good

When a friend of mine turned thirty, she was depressed for a week. I couldn't understand why she felt this way until she admitted that she felt like a failure in life. She and her husband were not getting along, and she knew they would eventually get a divorce. She felt as if she had spent the last few years running at full speed yet not moving forward, only digging herself into a life that made her very unhappy.

She made me realize how different a person views a birthday when you're happy with your life. When you live your life with no regrets and you're happy with the choices you've made, getting older is easier to accept.

This month I'll be forty. The big Four Oh! I don't feel older, but there is no denying the fact that I am getting older. Aging, so far, has been one of the best things about life. When I think about the person I was in my twenties, and I think about the person I am today, there is nothing that would make me want to be in my twenties again.

Aging gives us permission to stand up for ourselves. Maybe it's not so much "permission" as it is that by experiencing life we learn how to live better. I have become selfish with my time and spend it only with people I really want to be with. I'm learning to say no and not feel guilty about taking care of myself.

I'm at the stage in my life where I know—*really* know what I want out of life. I've learned that when we have no sense of purpose and meaning, we simply live a life but don't really *experience* life. We just go through the motion of living without really feeling alive.

In order to be happy, we have to believe in what we're doing, in the kind of life we're leading. Living life and truly opening up to all that life has to offer is scary. Starting a new job, a new relationship, having a family—everything is a risk. Accomplishing these things isn't easy, but unless we fight for our happiness and follow our hearts, we will never truly experience life.

It must be awful to reach old age and have a list of regrets and to look back at our life wishing we could have lived it differently. Life isn't always easy. We're not always happy. Sad things happen. It is precisely when we're going through tough times that we realize what happiness is and how precious our time on this earth is. We realize we shouldn't waste it.

Learning to love the new person that emerges after every birthday takes some getting use to. It's difficult to pinpoint exactly when we realize we are getting older. It just happens! One day we look in the mirror, and we see a wrinkle we hadn't seen before. Our bodies begin to change, and, no matter how much we work out, we just don't look the same.

Attitude clearly plays a major role throughout life and especially when you get older. It's crucial to realize that the important part of aging has nothing to do with our outer appearance, but it has to do with our inner life—how we define ourselves, how we feel about the person we have become.

All of us are aging all the time, and we don't think about it until the numbers begin to get larger. A midlife crisis happens when we haven't been true to ourselves.

Don't wait for happiness to find you. Happiness isn't a condition that descends upon you. It doesn't just bang you on the head and announce its arrival. We have to create it. We have to be honest with ourselves with our hopes and dreams.

Life is too precious to waste and too wonderful not to experience fully. If you're unhappy, don't wait for life to get better—make it better. Take control. Seize life!

WHY ARE WE SO UNHAPPY?

Sometimes it is embarrassing to live in the most comfortable time in history and still hear people complain. It is difficult to explain to people who have never lived outside the United States how wonderful life is here and how many opportunities we all have to reach our dreams and goals. Since I was born in another country, I have had the opportunity to see life from a different perspective. Experiencing life through the eyes of a Cuban immigrant has always kept me well grounded.

I left Cuba when I was four, and I didn't see my grandparents again until I was in my twenties. My paternal grandparents came to the United States in the 1980s around the time of the Mariel boat lift.

I will never forget how much pleasure my *abuelos* took out of small insignificant things. After living in a communist country for many years and getting by without so many of the conveniences we take for granted here, it was difficult for my grandparents to understand that they wouldn't run out of soap, shampoo, or food. It didn't seem possible that whenever they needed anything all they had to do was buy it at the grocery store.

Abuela Luisa loved sardines. But it had been so long since she'd eaten any that she couldn't remember what they tasted like. For the first few months in the United States, she must have eaten more sardines then any of us eat in a lifetime.

Once when I visited my grandparents' apartment, I noticed she had many empty plastic containers and glass jars under her sink. When I asked her about them, she told me she couldn't throw them away because she always thought about her friends back in Havana and how much they could use them.

We throw everything away without thinking, yet a glass jar in a communist country is a treasured possession. In the United States we buy water at the grocery store in plastic containers and milk sealed in cartons or plastic jugs. This luxury doesn't exist in Cuba. People will pay to obtain anything they can use to store food and water.

A grocery store as we know it doesn't exist for the Cuban people. Tourists visiting the island are the only people allowed to buy in the government-owned grocery stores.

Abuelo Chito was a very quiet man who needed very little to be happy. Whenever I think about him, I think about how much he enjoyed wearing the watch my father gave him when he arrived from Cuba. He never took it off. When the watch he owned in Cuba broke, he spent years without one. It's hard to believe that a watch could give a person so much pleasure.

My maternal grandmother, Abuela Nona, loved perfume and powder and pretty feminine clothing. After so many years without such luxuries, my mother and her four sisters spoiled Abuela. On Mother's Day or on her birthday, we would all go to her house. Abuela would be sitting in the middle of the room enjoying the attention. Everyone would bring her gifts, and she would always have her picture taken surrounded by all her presents.

Abuela would open her gifts as if she were savoring a delicious meal. She would pick up one at a time and look at the paper it was wrapped in. Then very slowly, without tearing the paper or the bow, she would open her presents, stacking paper, ribbons, and bows neatly to one side. She would never throw anything away.

Why are we so unhappy when we have it so good? The answer is simple. Our priorities are all messed up.

We don't take the time to appreciate pretty wrapping paper. Most people take America and the life they live for granted. Happiness could be standing right in front of them, but they have such a distorted view of life that they don't realize how blessed they are.

As parents of the future generation of Americans, we need to communicate with our children about what America is and has been and why this country deserves to be respected and loved. We need to remind our children that not everyone is as fortunate as they are, and that life as we know it is a privilege and a blessing we should never take for granted.

In With the New

The setting sun of an old year is the time to look back at what we have accomplished. Life sometimes takes us to unexpected places and the unexpected happens.

Whatever our personal plans may be, we should never lose sight of other people. We need to not only respect ourselves and what we stand for, but we should consider and care for other people.

When we make our New Year's resolutions, we need to think of *who* we are. Our success or failure depends upon who this person is. Resolutions do very little in the way of changing a person because they are easily made and easily broken.

I read once that we promise according to our hopes and perform according to our selfishness. When we don't keep a promise to others, it is a disappointment to those involved. But when we don't keep that promise to ourselves, we are only fooling ourselves.

We live in a world that has lost the thread that holds together the tapestry of everything important in life. Many marriages don't last, work and social commitments come before our children. Faithfulness, honesty, and respect are hard to come by.

We should all strive to be the kind of person who will always make time for a person in need of our love. We should all take the time to listen to our children, our spouse, and those closest to us who are often the ones we neglect the most.

We must always look for the joy in life and be ready for opportunities that life has a way of offering us, small gifts for which we should always be thankful.

From 1985 through 1990, I took writing courses just for the sake of learning the art of writing. Deep down inside I had always had this need to express myself through words. I am a romantic, and beautiful words have always moved me.

When I began writing, I never imagined where it would lead. In 1989, I sold my first article. I wrote it while sitting outside watching my sons play on the swings. For the next few years, I continued to write about motherhood and my experiences as a Cuban-American.

Writing was something I would squeeze into my schedule whenever I could. The older my sons became, however, the more time I had to write and the more it became a part of my life.

In 1994, *The Monitor* gave me the opportunity to share my work with my hometown. For the first time in years, not just my family and close friends would read something I had written. At first, I wondered how much of my life I could share. Would I be able to convey my sentiments to others, and would they understand me?

The amazing and wonderful thing has been the response I have gotten from the community. I have found that we are not that different after all, and that regardless of where we were born or what we do for a living, we are very much alike.

We are mothers and fathers, sons and daughters, husbands and wives, friends and lovers. We all share a common bond called life.

I am grateful for the gifts, cards, phone calls, and e-mails I have received over the years. Many of you have come up to me at the grocery store, restaurants, or social events and have told me how my column has touched you in some way. Some of you have shared very personal things with me, and your trust has been a gift I will always cherish.

A piece of my heart goes into every story I write, and I thank you for giving me the opportunity to share my life with you.

GIVE WHAT YOU CAN

I was in a hospital waiting room sitting with the family of a friend of mine. The surgeon had just informed her husband that everything had gone well. We were talking quietly when a woman approached me.

She was a social worker, and she needed someone to witness a man signing his living will. She had found two witnesses, but she needed one more. Everyone she had asked had turned her down.

She warned me that the man was very ill and that she would understand if I didn't want to do it. I hesitated for a moment; then I decided to go with her. I followed her down the hall where we met the other two volunteers, a woman in her fifties and a man in his twenties.

Before we entered the patient's room, the social worker explained the situation to us. This man had been diagnosed a few months ago with terminal cancer. Everything had happened very quickly, and he had somehow put off signing his living will.

She explained that a living will is a will in which the signer, in the event of terminal illness, requests to be allowed to die rather than be kept alive by medical life-support systems. If he didn't sign this will soon, he would be going into a coma and his family would not be able to carry out his wishes.

The patient lay on the hospital bed. His face was pale, and he wore an oxygen mask. On one side of his bed was his wife and on the other side stood his daughter. Their faces wore months of pain and sadness.

The social worker asked us to stand at the foot of the bed. She handed the papers to his daughter who placed them in front of her father. His daughter held him up while his wife held his hand.

He would open his eyes and try to focus, but with his first few attempts he just fell back exhausted with the effort. They urged him to sign.

His wife and daughter were in tears by the time he finally signed the papers. I was trying not to cry, but I couldn't hold it in anymore, and I had to turn away. That's when I realized the woman and young man were crying, too.

We signed some papers. The other two witnesses shook hands with the wife and daughter and quickly left the room. I gave his wife a hug, and then I hugged his daughter.

We held each other and cried. I felt her pain as if it were my own. It was one of the saddest experiences I have ever had. When I left the room, I walked over to the water fountain. The social worker asked me if I was all right. I nodded, still unable to speak.

After I composed myself, I asked the social worker how she could do this every day and go home at night to her family without it affecting her. I couldn't imagine witnessing such pain on a daily basis.

She said at first it had been very difficult for her. For awhile she thought she wouldn't be able to do her job. Then one day, she realized that someone had to help these patients deal with their illnesses and help the families cope with their loss. Over the years, she had met incredibly brave people who face death with courage. They had taught her a lot about life.

When I left the hospital that afternoon, I couldn't help thinking how often we avoid certain situations because of how uncomfortable it makes us feel. Throughout life, God gives us many opportunities to reach out in small ways and give a bit of ourselves to help others.

Sometimes God teaches us through the pain of others. If we can help someone, and our acts can still be remembered after we're gone, then we have lived a meaningful life.

Happiness Should be Guilt Free

My Spanish culture loves to suffer. If you don't believe me, watch a Spanish soap opera. You don't have to understand Spanish to see the drama. In Cuba during my grandmother's time, women were expected to experience guilt. Guilt made you a better person. It showed you cared and that you were sensitive.

My mother was raised with many duties and responsibilities. I've never been exposed to the guilt she felt whenever she didn't do something that was expected of her. When she raised us, she didn't impose all those unnecessary traditions.

In her own way, mother became somewhat liberated without totally losing her Cuban customs. She became more independent, and my parents enjoyed the freedom of living their lives without the constraints their families sometimes put on them.

One of the most important lessons we can teach our children is to model how to be happy in life. Teach them how to make the most out of every single day and not let anyone or anything ruin their day.

Teach them how to be content and grateful for what they have and always be happy for others. Some people have everything they could possibly need to be happy but are so preoccupied with what others have, they fail to see how blessed they are.

Happiness has to come from within us. It's in our smile, our laughter, our hugs and all the things we do for our family and friends.

Happiness is accepting ourself as a woman, a wife, a mother, and not the perfect super person we think we ought to be.

Happiness is free, and you can have as much as you want. Learn how to look for those special moments in life and hold them close to your heart. Let happiness become a positive ray of light that spills around everything and everyone with whom you come into contact.

Summertime Memories

"The happiest moments of my life have been
the few which I have passed at home in the bosom
of my family."[2] Thomas Jefferson

Summertime means being able to spend time with
my children without having to worry about schedules.
I miss those uncomplicated years when nothing was
more important that sitting outside watching them play
on the swings.

When I was a little girl, I loved summer vacation.
During the last week of school at Field's Elementary
School, I'd sit at my desk slumped in my seat; my
teacher's voice and the humming of the fan made me
sleepy.

A hot breeze swirled around the room, and I would
look out the window and daydream of the coming
summer months. Today, life is so hectic that most children will never enjoy the lazy summer months my
brother and I enjoyed.

I remember hot summer nights when we'd sit out on
the porch of our little house after dinner. My brother
and I took turns sharing stories, and my parents talked
about their goals and dreams.

Sometimes the four of us sat quietly, each lost in his
or her own thoughts, enjoying the peacefulness of the
night, listening to the sound of the crickets. I'd grow
sleepy feeling safe, content with the knowledge that life
couldn't be any better.

In the backyard of our first house stood a magnifi-
cent old oak tree. Its limbs were long, reaching out
across the yard, shading us from the hot summer sun.
My mother would sit and read, and I would lie on the

cool grass next to her, looking up at the clouds peeking between the branches.

The tree sheltered many birds. I could hear them chirping cheerfully, safely nestled in the strong branches. Every so often, sparrows darted in and out of the tree, chasing each other.

Those were long hot summer days when time seemed to crawl by and life was simple and sweet. William Blake, the poet, believed that if man kept alive his ability to see and feel the reality of life, his menial tasks would become easy.

Life never stands still, but we have today—today we can enjoy life. Nothing could be sadder than the parent who never spends time with his children, and then one day wakes up and realizes he has missed the opportunity to build the bridges of understanding that only happen with daily doses of love.

Enjoy the time you have with your children, and spend some lazy summer days under an old oak tree. Enjoy the flowers at your feet and the children who eventually will grow up and find their separate path.

Disco Night

The other night my husband and I went out with my brother and his wife. A new club opened in McAllen, and my brother had received an invitation to its grand opening.

Whenever we go out with my brother and his wife, it always reminds us of when we were newlyweds. All we thought about was each other, and we did not have to worry about the commitments and obligations that come with raising a family.

My brother has kept us young. I say this because, until April of this year, he was a bachelor. For years he's been our social organizer, keeping us busy with invitations to social functions and planning fun things to do.

My husband and I love to go out. When we're in McAllen, however, we get so caught up with work and family commitments that we tend not to go out on dates as much as we would like to.

As parents, it's not easy to disconnect from our parenting mode. The weekend rolls around and our teenage children make plans with their friends. By the time our house is empty, we're so grateful for the peace and quiet that we'd rather stay home.

When we go out of town, we always go dancing. In large cities, nightclubs are filled with people of all ages. In the Valley, the regulars at most clubs are in their twenties and thirties, or at least that's the age everyone appeared to us last week. When we're at a nightclub and most of the people there look young enough to be our children, it makes us feel a hundred years old.

When we entered the club with my brother, all his bachelor friends came to say hello. Many of them had wondered what had happened to him since they didn't know he had gotten married.

The flashing lights and the music got me in a good mood.

"Let me know when you want to dance," my husband said to me.

But I never got the urge. Instead, I was content just to sit and watch everyone else having a good time. Thirty minutes later the much-anticipated band from Mexico City began to play. We were looking forward to hearing some good music. After listening to the singer a few minutes, my husband turned to me and asked, "What language is he singing in?"

"It's Spanish." I answered.

"I can't understand a word he's saying."

"Me neither," I said as we looked at each other and began to laugh hysterically.

My twenty-eight-year-old sister-in-law, on the other hand, knew all the words to the songs, and she was singing to my brother. In fact, everywhere we looked, people were dancing and singing to Spanish rock.

"Do you realize what's happening to us?" I asked my husband.

"Yes," he said. "We're getting old."

After about 45 minutes of trying to decipher the words the young man was singing, I looked at my watch. It was only 11:30. If we returned home, I could help our son study for his anatomy test.

"You see that sign over there," my husband said as he pointed to one of those electronic signs that flashes messages. "They misspelled 'discover.'" I looked over at the sign and the words flashed by.

"You're right," I said. Then I glanced at the sign again and realized it read DISCO BAR. We both laughed so hard we almost fell off the bar stools.

That was the sign we needed to realize it was time to leave. We said good-bye to my brother and his wife and headed home. As we were getting into the car, I glanced at the back seat. Staring back at me was my daughter's doll; next to it lay a Dr. Seuss book and the Goofy hat she had worn to school for hat day.

"This is our life," I said pointing to the back seat.

"It's great, isn't it!" my husband said, as we drove home holding hands.

Every stage in life is special. But the most important stage will always be the one you're living now. When you have someone to share your life with, getting older means life just keeps on getting better.

SHARE YOUR STORIES

I love to listen to stories, especially those told by the older generation. We learn so much about life by listening to these wise human beings talk about all the things they've been through in life.

Most of us have grown up hearing stories about how our parents met. We've heard our parents talk about hurricanes they've been through and disastrous vacations. These stories connected to childhood memories are very much a part of each of us.

Stories have helped me learn about life. They have taught me about adversity and how a family can survive difficult times. Certain stories are so important, they deserve to be told over and over again.

At our family gatherings it's not uncommon to hear talk of how life used to be in Cuba. I can sit for hours and listen to my relatives. They bring life to my Cuban past, and I relish these special stories that help keep my Cuban traditions alive.

When I was little, I used to love to spend the night at my aunts' house. They would tell me stories about their childhood, oftentimes sharing incidents my mother had forgotten.

When my cousins and I were growing up, my aunts told us stories whenever they wanted to give us advice.

Hundreds of years ago before books were popular, people passed their knowledge, family history, songs, and customs by telling stories.

Today we live life in a rush; families live far apart. Friendships are hard to hold onto when careers move us to different parts of the country. Work, television, and computers have changed our lives.

Unimportant schedules and activities are stealing our lives and we're losing precious time. We are so busy we are missing beautiful sunsets and all those things that make life worth living.

Stories transcend time and distance and give depth and meaning to family time. Family is all about memories and love. We need to make time for our children.

Generations from now, one of your stories might bring to life the happiness you're sharing with your family today.

CHAPTER OPENED BY A CHANCE ENCOUNTER

Every convention you can imagine is held in Las Vegas. It's a good place to work and have fun at the same time.

My husband and I go to Las Vegas at least once a year. I always attend the conventions with him, but on a recent trip I decided to stay in our room and work on my book. Every day about the same time a lovely woman would come to clean my room. She was very friendly, and she was always humming.

The first day she came to my room she was shy, but eventually she began to talk to me. She was curious as to why she found me sitting in front of my computer every day, instead of gambling or shopping.

I told her that I was a writer and that I was trying to finish my book.

"You write about me?" she said with a grin. "But, I no tell you my name."

"Where are you from?" I asked her.

"I am born in Somalia."

"Why won't you tell me your name?"

"I afraid," she said. "I always afraid, the afraid never go away."

I understood her fear. When my aunts first came from Cuba, they were always afraid to talk negatively about Castro or anything that had happened in Cuba. They would always whisper. It took years for them to be able to talk freely without the fear that someone would overhear their conversation.

My nameless friend came to this country with her husband when she was twenty-six years old. A family from North Dakota sponsored them and helped them get started. When I told her I was Cuban, she smiled and in her beautiful accent said, "You understand me. Yes?"

In Somalia, she witnessed her sister being killed and many of her friends tortured. She missed her country, but not the government that is torturing and killing so many innocent people.

"Bad government in my country," she said. "Just like Castro."

We talked while she changed the sheets on my bed. Every once in awhile, when she would talk about something painful, she would stop and wipe away the tears from her eyes.

In Somalia, she was tortured for being a Christian. First she showed me a scar on her hand. Then she said, "I want to show you something, OK?"

She pulled up her blouse and showed me her stomach. It was covered with horrendous scars.

"They torture me," she said. "They cut my stomach and cut my tubes, so that I can never make baby. This is why I can never be happy. I work. I eat, but for what. No baby."

I didn't know what to say and then she gave me a sad smile and said, "I made you sad. Yes?"

"Yes," I said. "I'm sorry that you have had to go through so much."

"I sorry, too," she said sadly. "American people lucky, they no understand. They free to make great life. They have great country."

"I agree," I said. "Americans have no idea what some people have to go through to have the kind of freedom Americans take for granted."

"Lady, you tell my story, yes? Make a Somalian woman famous."

"Yes, I'll write your story."

"No name!" she said, covering her name tag.

"No name," I said.

As she closed the door to my room, I sat down in front of my computer to write everything down. I didn't want to forget the way she spoke, the way she expressed herself.

I believe that God puts people in our path for a reason. I am certain that it wasn't an accident that this lovely woman cleaned my room. She had something to say, and I had the means to share her sad story.

SECTION II

A MOTHER'S LOVE

Thank Goodness for Motherhood

Motherhood is not a profession you can learn about in a book. It's not something you inherit from your mother like beautiful hair or strong nails.

For some women, motherhood is an overwhelming responsibility. For others, it is a natural stepping stone to another phase in their life. Regardless of how you feel about motherhood, once you become a mother it is a lifetime commitment.

I was raised in a family by a mother whose existence was centered in motherhood. There is something very comforting about knowing you are loved in this way. It is like always having a soft blanket of love. You know it's there whether you need it or not.

When I was little, I loved to play dolls. When I got older, I loved to be around children. I am happiest when I am mothering someone, a trait my younger brother didn't always appreciate when we were growing up.

My oldest son made a difficult entry into the world. After twenty-four hours of labor, he burst into my life looking like a boxer. He had forceps marks on his face and body, and one eye was swollen shut.

The moment they placed him on my stomach bundled in a blanket, I felt a deep love that comes with holding your firstborn. Two years later, when I became pregnant again, I wondered how I would be able to have enough love to share with another baby.

When my second son was born and placed into my arms, I held the most beautiful baby I had ever seen. Again I experienced that unique kind of love that links a woman with her baby.

Thirteen years later, I am once again a mother—this time of a beautiful daughter whose arrival in our lives has blessed us with joy. It has been wonderful after all these years to cherish holding a baby in my arms. When she calls me Mimi or Mami, her sweet voice amazes me.

I have become selfish with my time. I find the weeks slipping past me without having accomplished much of anything. Stacks of unfinished articles, short stories, and unread books lie on my desk. The wonderful thing about it is, I don't feel guilty!

I am enjoying this very special holding time with my eighteen-month-old daughter. It's a short period when babies seem to always want to be in your arms. I love the feeling of having her warm little body on my hip. She is the daughter of my dreams.

I look at my children with gratitude and wonder. I am the mother of three very special individuals who radiate a warm feeling, from which I draw strength and courage. My firstborn taught me to be a mother. With him I learned to give unselfishly of my love. My second son guided me into maturity, and I have learned from being his mother.

My daughter is a bright star sent from heaven whose existence fills my heart with awe-inspiring love. The most important accomplishment in my life are my children. They are the core and source of all that matter and are important to me.

I am eternally grateful that God chose me to be their mother.

Children are Parents' Greatest Masterpiece

As parents, our role is similar to that of a sculptor. Every day we slowly help to mold the kind of person our child will become in the future. But unlike the sculptor, our work never ends; it is a lifetime commitment.

The influence we have on a child is an overwhelming responsibility. I have always been an optimistic person, and I know it is due to the positive influence my parents had on me.

When I was four years old, my family emigrated from Cuba. As a child, I grew up with very little in terms of material goods. Times were tough and my parents constantly struggled to better themselves and learn the language of their new home.

My mother has often told me how she and my father promised each other never to make our lives miserable by grieving over how different life might have been had Castro not taken over Cuba.

As parents, sometimes we unintentionally complicate our children's lives with our problems, our frustrations with work, and our resentments toward other people. Children pick up the negative part of our attitude as well as the positive. Every morning without realizing it, we set the mood for their day. Children take their cue from us.

When I was growing up, I never felt poor or deprived. I remember coming home from school every day to find the dining room set with a pretty tablecloth. There was always something delicious to eat, and we would sit down and have a *merienda*.

I look back on those afternoons and think of them as brainwashing sessions for future references. The older my brother and I got, the more serious our conversations became. Day by day, little by little, my mother instilled in us a determination to succeed and a strong faith in God.

Without nagging or arguing, she made us realize the importance of education. She made us feel proud of who we were and taught us the importance of a family. We learned to enjoy and share in each others' accomplishments no matter how insignificant they might have been.

Together we worked to solve our problems, and most of the time what seemed an impossible situation became simple when we tackled the problem as a family.

Childhood only comes once in life, and it is those first few years that mold each of us into what we will become someday.

In every facet of our lives we must strive to show our children how to live and solve their problems with optimism and faith in God. With patience and love, we can help them accomplish whatever their dreams might be.

PASSING ON THE LOVE OF MY MOTHER

In the mornings after my sons leave for school and my husband has left for work, I'll pour myself a cup of coffee and sit in my kitchen reading the paper. My daughter always comes and sits on the stool next to me.

"Mami, can I have some coffee?" she asked me the other day. I poured some warm milk into a mug and a drop of coffee—just enough to make the milk look darker—and handed it to her. We sat there for awhile quietly enjoying our morning coffee when she turned to me and said, "*Somos dos amigas tomando café.*" We're two friends drinking coffee.

"Yes we are," I said, leaning over and giving her a kiss on the forehead.

Already at age four my daughter understands that although I'm her Mami I can also be her friend. Many mothers and daughters don't get along. They love each other, but somehow they never really get to know each other.

A child has no sense of what her relationship with her mother should be like. As the adult, each of us must reach out towards our child. It's up to us to develop a close relationship with our daughters.

When I think back on my childhood, I can remember my mother always being there for me, not only during important events in my life but on a daily basis in small ways.

One of my favorite things to do as a child was to sit on the kitchen counter and watch my mother cook. We would have wonderful conversations with the soft chirping of the pressure cooker in the background and the smell of black bean soup seeping from the pot.

When my parents came from Cuba, we could not afford to buy our clothes so my mother had no choice but to learn how to sew. I can still picture her in front of her sewing machine with the dining room table covered with patterns and different colored fabric. On Saturdays she would always have something simple for me to do. She taught me how to mend my clothes, and I learned about life from all of our long talks.

It was during one of these sewing sessions that I told my mother I was curious about smoking. A few minutes later we were in her car driving towards the grocery store where she bought a pack of cigarettes. We spent the rest of the morning sewing and smoking. I spent the time coughing and trying to act grown up with a cigarette in my mouth. We laughed and giggled at how silly we looked, and I lost interest in smoking. After all, if I could smoke with my mom, smoking didn't seem quite so exciting.

My mother has always known when to be my mother and when to be my friend. Unless you allow your daughter to know you as a person, you will never be able to develop a close relationship with her.

When a young girl has a good relationship with her mother, she gains a lifelong friend. Mothers give sustenance and courage to their daughters. The nurturing you receive from your mother is the thread that holds together generations of families.

Where would I have found maternal wisdom if I hadn't had my mother by my side guiding me through the stages of motherhood?

When I look at my daughter and think of all the things she will have to go through in life, I can't imagine not being by her side. What I feel for my daughter—the love that pours from my heart whenever I hold her or whenever she looks at me with innocence and trust—must be what my mother feels for me.

From my mother I have learned that the bridges of love must be built from the first moment you hold your child. A mother-daughter relationship is not something built from a quick kiss or an occasional hug, but from daily love and understanding. God has blessed me with a daughter, a sweet little girl who will someday grow up to be a mother. I will pass on to her all the love her grandmother has always shown me. Within her, my mother's love will live on.

I love you, *Mima*!

LEARN TO LOVE THE TEEN YEARS

When our oldest son turned thirteen, I looked forward to his teenage years instead of dreading them as some parents do. I think parents have a lot to do with teenage rebellion. If we would learn to relax and enjoy each stage in our child's life, our relationship with them would be less strained and more fulfilling.

Many parents blame the child who is becoming a teenager for the problems in the relationship. If we are not close to our children, how can we expect them to confide in us when they get older? That trust has to be cultivated over the years; it doesn't just happen overnight.

It is only natural that a teenager becomes more independent and begins to find interests of his or her own. This is an important part of growing up.

Treat your teenager as you would treat another adult. Cultivate a special bond with your child. Treat him or her with respect, courtesy, and love. Be a parent, but also be a friend.

Learn to talk to your teenager, instead of lecturing. Avoid criticizing and be sensitive when talking about his friends. I've always been honest with my son about what I think. If I don't like someone he is hanging around with, I tell him what bothers me about that person. But I have never made fun of or put down any of his friends.

Decide what is important and argue only about those issues. When you do argue, avoid losing your temper. If you stay in control, you will be able to communicate your feelings much more effectively, and you'll help your teenager stay calm.

When you are angry, never say things you will regret. This will only push your child further away from you.

Be affectionate and show your teenager you love him. Why should you stop hugging and kissing your child because he's getting older? There are times when a hug can express much more than words.

As a teenager, I used to curl up next to my father and watch TV. Sometimes, I'd pretend to be asleep so he would carry me to my room.

We never grow out of needing love from our parents. It doesn't matter how old I am—I know I can always call on my parents. Their unconditional love has made me a stronger person.

My sons are my special friends. I watch their programs and listen to their music. And when we talk, I listen with my heart and try to understand everything they are feeling.

Life is too short, and before long they will be grown men. They'll get married and have children of their own. The life cycle will begin all over again. And I want to be a part of their lives through each and every stage. Their love makes me look forward to the future, to knowing the kind of men they will become.

PINK GERMS

A few weeks ago my five-year-old daughter came home from preschool talking about germs. Her teacher did such a good job of explaining germs to her that for the rest of the week anytime we'd ask for a sip of her juice, she would immediately pull her glass away.

"No, Mami, you have germs."

"It's OK," I explained. "As long as no one is sick, we can share our food because we are a family and our germs get along. They're like brothers and sisters—we all have different germs, but we can all live in the same house."

"No, Mami, that's not right," she said. "My teacher said my germs can only be mine."

"Why is that?" I asked her.

"Because I'm a girl, and my germs are pink!"

"If your germs are pink, then what color germs does your Papi have?"

"Green," she said with a giggle and then proceeded to explain the germ theory to us. I have pink germs because I'm a girl like her. Her brothers have orange germs, her grandparents have white germs, and PeeWee, my oldest son's kitten, has pink germs because my daughter likes him.

"How do you know what color germs everyone has?" I asked.

"Because my teacher tells me," she said.

Wow, different color germs! How different the world would be if everything could be the shade of color we chose it to be. Children can make the everyday world full of wonder and mystery; they can make the most ordinary things seem magical.

Small children live in the timelessness of the present. They have no worries, no responsibilities. Life is one long joyful ride. They just hop on without worrying where it will take them.

They can spend hours playing with their favorite toy or swinging high into the air. They are like little mystics who can travel easily between the visible and invisible worlds. They haven't been exposed to the boundaries of time and space. They always look for the rainbow and seldom worry about the storm. Once we're adults, it seems we spend our life preparing for the storm.

We worry about our families and sometimes about things that never come to be.

Maybe if we all just relaxed and kept an open mind, we'd fine it easier to solve our problems.

As adults we can't pretend things are what we want them to be, but sometimes we have to open ourselves up to all the possibilities that do exist. We need to view life through a wide-angle scope so that we don't miss all that is around us.

Sometimes we get so caught up with finding a purpose to everything we do, we forget to ask ourselves why we're doing it. Children live life with a source of wisdom and love that most of us lose in the process of getting older.

Pink is my daughter's favorite color so everything in her life is pink. I feel responsible for the role the color pink plays in her life. After two sons, I looked forward to cute frilly pink outfits. No blue, no yellow; only pink. Maybe I overdid it!

Nevertheless, if she believes her germs are pink—let her. Soon enough she'll realize life is not always made of the shades of color we wish. Life has many different stages filled with vivid colors, some darker than others.

Born to be Friends

We all need friendships. We all need that deep connection with another person. As most of us know, however, acquaintances are many but real friends are few. We're lucky if we can count them on one hand.

I've always told my sons that besides their father and me, the only other people they will be able to count on in life is each other and their sister. "Brothers do not fight." They've heard this over and over again throughout their childhood, as well as how important it is that they look out for each other.

Now that they are both grown, I talk to them about the responsibility they have to watch over their little sister. This is part of belonging to a family.

A family loves and respects each other. Siblings should be able to trust each other, to be loving critics as well as to be emotionally available, supportive, and encouraging towards each other.

When my brother and I would fight, my mother would punish us by making us sit side by side in a corner of the dining room. Then she would tell us how lucky we were to have each other and how important it was for brothers and sisters to get along.

If we were arguing, we were not allowed to get up from our chairs until we had apologized to each other and given each other a hug and a kiss. Without realizing it, mother made us grow up thinking of each other not only as brother and sister but also as friends.

My brother and I had our usual sibling fights. But most of the time there was love and appreciation between us. The older I get, the more I realize how lucky I am to have a friend in my brother. He is someone I can trust and count on. He is someone I can go to, who loves me and cares about my family as much as I do.

There has never been jealousy between us, and as adults I can't remember ever arguing with him. We trust each other, respect each other, and our bond as brother and sister can never be severed. I wouldn't allow it, and I know he wouldn't either.

Parents play a major role in the relationship siblings have with each other. By accepting their children's fights, rivalry, and jealousies as part of a normal sibling relationship, they're not teaching their children to treat their siblings as they would treat a friend.

Many parents put more emphasis on the importance of being nice to others than they do on how important it is that their own children get along. Instead of teaching their children how to enjoy spending time together, they allow them to bring home friends to keep them entertained. Having friends over is fine, but your children should also be able to get along with each other, too. They should be able to communicate with each other, to enjoy watching a movie together or attending a family outing without arguing.

It is important to have family time. Spending time together will give your children the opportunity to talk to each other about things that are happening in their lives. In order for your children to be friends, they must understand each other and accept their differences. Sibling rivalry or jealousy should not be thought of as funny and something that will go away as your children become older. Sometimes parents allow it to go too far, and it severs the relationship their children have with each other.

We need to teach our children to respect each other. Teach them that, in friendship, secrets can be told and heard and should never be repeated. Conversations that take place at home are private; teach your children this at a young age.

A sibling can be your closest friend, the one person other than your parents who understands the person you really are. A child's relationship with a sibling is a unique bond that is based on shared experiences.

Teach your children to love each other, help them cultivate a close relationship with their siblings. Siblings can learn from and learn with each other as they journey through life.

Golden Link Binds Mother and Child

"A mother's love is indeed the golden link that binds youth to age; and he is still but a child, however time may have furrowed his cheek, or silvered his brow, who can yet recall, with a softened heart, the fond devotion, or the gentle chiding, of the best friend that God ever gives us."[3]

I am blessed to have a mother whose love and support I have always been able to count on. Over the years she has not only been my mother, she's been my best friend.

During my teens, when most of my friends were arguing with their mothers, I was enjoying a loving relationship with mine. I have always been able to tell her everything, even things that most moms and daughter don't discuss.

Mother has always known when to be my mother and when to be my friend. She has spent her whole life dedicated to her family. Her unselfishness, her love for us, and her support toward my father have set high standards for my life.

My mother's happy, positive attitude has helped our family make it through rough times. My brother and I have always been the recipients of her spontaneous touch, hugs, kisses, and the warmth that has always radiated from her smile.

She raised us with a firm but very loving hand. She taught us to have faith in God, about right and wrong, and of justice and morals.

Throughout every stage in our life, our mother has been a source of encouragement. She has invested her time and energy in helping us fulfill our potential.

The feminist movement has taught us how women need challenges and satisfaction in life. Many women search for these things outside the home, never realizing that they are missing out on the most important job in life.

Staying home and raising our children fills us with a spiritual satisfaction, a feeling of wholeness that only motherhood can provide. Being a mother is doing the most important job on earth. It's taking the life of a human being, creating and shaping it for the future.

We can all return to careers, but we can never go back to watching our children grow. Those tender moments are far too short and precious to miss out on.

Throughout my whole life, I have felt loved and wanted. I know that regardless how old I am, I can always count on my mother's advice and comforting hugs.

Since the birth of my children, Mother has been a devoted grandmother, helping me with car pools, birthday parties, and chicken pox. She has laughed at her grandchildrens' mischievous stunts, claiming grandmothers are supposed to be fun.

Whatever my children have needed, she has provided. But most of all my children know that, no matter what, Abuela will always be there.

The most beautiful gift my mother has given me is her love, and for as long as I live I will be grateful that God chose her for me.

CELEBRATING THE MIRACLE OF LIFE

As I write this, my nine-month-old daughter is playing happily in her playpen next to my desk. She's dressed in a soft pink cotton jumper trimmed with lace, and sitting on her tiny head is a very tiny bow.

Every time I look at her, she squeals and I am rewarded with a beautiful smile. She is our miracle, and my heart is overwhelmed with love for this baby who has blessed our lives with so much happiness.

Babies remind me of the miracle of life. In my twenties I embraced motherhood with exuberance; young and inexperienced, I never worried about anything. I was invincible and life was hectic and wonderful with my little boys.

That time came and went much too quickly, and between baby bottles and diapers the months and years flew by. Being a mother at the age of thirty-six is different—it's sweeter than it was before. My love for this baby is no different from the love I felt for my sons. But at ages twenty and twenty-two, I took having a baby for granted.

Now I am in awe by every facet of motherhood—by the extraordinary experience of being pregnant and having a child. And by the wonder of adoption, one woman giving another the most precious gift of all—a life.

My daughter has reminded me of little things I had forgotten. Cradling her, a serene softness spills through me. It's something about holding a tiny life that makes you feel gentle...maternal.

I am once again enjoying the silky feel of a baby's skin, the warmth of her head when I place my chin next to her, and the contagious sound of her laughter when I tickle her. I had forgotten the peaceful look on a baby's face when she is sound asleep, oblivious to the world around her.

On those special nights when only my daughter and I are awake and I am rocking her to sleep, she looks up at me with her beautiful dark brown eyes. I am overcome with emotion and with the precious gift God has given us.

Motherhood gives us a lifetime gift by giving us the opportunity to fall in love with our children over and over again. With every stage our child enters, a different person emerges and our relationship changes.

Regardless of how old they become, every once in a while, when we look at them, we are reminded of the first time we held them.

Having a baby sister has shown my sons how much love and care it takes to raise a child. They understand now how it feels to look at this innocent baby and realize how much she depends on us. They will watch their little sister grow up and will understand why we love them as much as we do.

Our house, which has always been a male-dominated household, finally has another female to help me straighten out the men. I'm looking forward to having company when the men go off on hunting and fishing trips. Along with basketballs, baseball bats, and baseball gloves, our house will have ballet slippers and baby dolls.

I finally have someone who will help me decorate Christmas cookies, who will go shopping with me and will someday accompany me to mushy movies the men never want to go see.

I look forward to every stage of her life. Much too soon, my daughter will be all grown up, and I will have the best friend a mother could ever ask for. But now I am content to watch her quietly as she sleeps, cherishing this moment—the life we share, and the joy she's brought our family.

The Passing of Time

As the new school year approaches and another wonderful summer is gone, I can't help but feel a bit sad. Summers seem to get shorter, and I often wish I could make them last longer.

When we're young, we don't realize how fast time goes by. Instead, we're always waiting for some milestone—becoming a teenager, getting a driver's license, high school graduation. It's only when you're older that you wish you could slow things down.

Not too long ago the beginning of school meant buying crayons, pencils, construction paper, and new backpacks. I miss those years most; I miss having little boys.

My older son is a senior this year. One night he went to bed a young boy and the next morning, he woke up a man. I don't know where the time has gone, but I can feel it slipping by me even as I write. Next year around this time he'll be getting ready for his first year of college. And I will begin a new stage in my life, one I'm not sure I'm ready for.

It seems only yesterday he was a freshman at Memorial High School. Two weeks after school started, I received a phone call from a senior girl. A group of seniors were organizing an initiation ceremony for freshmen. She wanted my permission to kidnap my son. The plan was that the seniors would kidnap the freshmen early in the morning, dress them up in used clothing, and parade them around town. She promised all the pranks would be in good fun, and he would get to school on time.

My first instinct was to say no and play it safe, but I knew my son would want to be initiated along with his friends. At 4:30 A.M. on a Thursday, I led a group of seniors to my son's room. They woke him up, took his picture, and dragged him out the door.

After they left I tried going back to sleep, but I could hear the cars driving up and down our street. I finally got up and stood out on my bedroom balcony. The seniors' meeting place was across some empty lots at a neighbor's house.

It was dark, and I knew no one could see me. I, on the other hand, had a great view of the initiation party. The street was filled with cars and our neighbor's front yard was crowded with teenagers.

One group of freshmen was singing a silly song. Another group was doing some kind of funny dance. From the back yard, you could hear the girls scream-ing—then a splash as another group was thrown in the pool. It was chaotic and crazy, and the morning air was filled with laughter.

It was at this precise moment that I realized my son had grown up. As the cars drove off one by one, I felt as if a piece of his childhood was also slowly leaving me behind.

Teary-eyed, I watched the morning sun show its first rays of light. Today's initiation had really been mine, not my son's. I realized that from now on there would be times I wouldn't know where he was or what he was doing. There would be parties, dates, and spring break. I would have to learn how to start letting go.

As a mother, whenever I see youth enjoying them-selves, I always say a prayer. I remember being that innocent, thinking nothing could ever happen to me. I miss being that carefree and, to a point, I wish we could all hold on to it. But as an adult, I know how dangerous that euphoria can be if we never outgrow that stage.

At 8:30 A.M. the doorbell rang and there stood my son dressed in bright yellow baggy pants and a striped shirt two sizes too small. The school had sent some of the freshmen home to change.

His body was covered with flour and someone had drawn a heart on each cheek. He had a hug pacifier hanging from his neck and a cardboard sign that read "I love sin." His brown eyes shone and his smile filled my heart with joy. I could tell he had passed his initiation, but would I be able to pass mine?

This Son of Mine

In a few weeks, my oldest son will graduate from Memorial High School. I look at this 6-foot-2-inch, 18-year-old man, and it's hard to believe he is my little boy. I can still remember the night he was born. I was in labor for twenty-four hours before he decided to join our family. He was a big baby weighing 8-1/2 pounds and measuring 20-1/2 inches long.

When the nurse placed him on my stomach bundled in his blanket, he looked like a boxer with his left eye swollen shut. He was sucking his hand hungrily, and it had a red mark from having been doing so all through my pregnancy.

I felt an overwhelming passion holding this child for the first time. An immediate bond was formed between us, a special love that comes from being the firstborn. I felt blessed that God had given me the privilege of becoming a mother.

There are memories of those first few days with him that I will never forget. The look on my husband's face the first time he held his son. My mother hiding in the bathroom so that she could hold her grandson when the nurse brought him to me for his feedings.

My son didn't let me sleep much the first year of his life, often waking up in the middle of the night for a bottle. As a toddler, he was very active and funny, always laughing a great deal. He was affectionate, lovable, and very generous with his hugs and kisses.

On his fifth birthday as we sang happy birthday, he stood beaming behind his G.I. Joe cake. I felt a lump in my throat. My son was five years old. Where had the time gone?

He was a sweet little boy with an exuberant personality. He often did things that would touch my heart. I remember one afternoon, exhausted after a hectic morning, I fell asleep on the sofa while he watched cartoons.

I woke up when I felt two little hands tucking a blanket under my chin. "It's OK, Mami. Go back to sleep. It's only me." Then placing his soft, chubby hands on my cheeks, he gently kissed my forehead. Quietly, he went back and sat in front of the television.

Our relationship has always been like this. My gifts of love have never gone unnoticed. And they have always been returned with the same unselfishness and loving devotion with which they were given.

On his 13th birthday, I wrote him a letter. I wanted him to know how it felt to be a mother of a teenager. I wanted him to understand that there would be times we would disagree, but no matter what took place between us, I loved him and would always be there for him.

It has always been difficult me for me to say no to him. His devilish smile and charming nature remind me so much of his father. Even when he's done something wrong, I can't stay angry at him for very long.

Once again, I find myself entering another stage in my son's life. My eyes fill with tears often these days, tears of joy, tears of longing for my little boy. I find myself hugging him more than usual.

When he puts his arms around me and places his chin on my head, I am aware of the awesome gift God has given me. His love radiates a warm feeling from which I draw strength. Someday our roles will change. I see that now. He will watch over me. He will be there to hold my hand and comfort me just as I have done for him.

On graduation night, I will be at the stadium watching the class of 1998 graduate; my heart will be filled with pride. I know my son has the strength and the heart and mind to accomplish whatever he dreams of doing.

I'm excited for him and all the wonderful experiences he has to look forward to in life. It's tough letting go—it's a delicate process of letting go of my little boy and still holding onto his heart.

I'm looking forward to the beginning of a new stage in our relationship. I know that regardless of how far away from me he is, our love will always hold us together. We will always share a powerful bond, a deep love, a oneness…only a mother and son can understand.

All in a Day's Work

In a corner of my office my four-year-old daughter has a Little Tyke desk. On her desk she has an old computer keyboard. She has a drawer full of markers, colors, and a notebook very similar to the one in which I use to keep my notes.

When I work, she works, too. Most of the time she'll let me write, interrupting me only occasionally for a quick hug and a kiss. Some days, however, she wants more than that and those are the days it's very difficult to get anything done.

A few days ago while I was working, my daughter insisted on typing the letter M on the computer. M is the first letter of her name and, of course, her favorite letter. I explained that I was working but that as soon as I was through I would show her how to type her whole name.

"Show me now," she said, putting her arms around my neck and crawling up on my lap. Positioning her little hands on the keyboard, she looked up innocently. I took a deep breath and reminded myself to be *patient*.

Sometimes I wish patience were something I could buy at the grocery store and stock in my pantry. It would make my life so much easier if I could spice up my meals with it, sprinkling it over everything I ate.

After ten long minutes of writing her name. I convinced my daughter to let me work and off she went. I looked at my watch and by then it was already 6:00 P.M. I had only thirty more minutes left to write before it was time for her bath.

Women of my generation have always been told we can do it all. Most of us know that it isn't quite that simple. Whether you work outside your home or you're a stay-at-home mom, a woman's job never ends.

There are days when juggling it all seems easy. Then there are days when I feel I'm being pulled in different directions, and it's overwhelming. Most of us, when given a choice, will always choose our families first. Whatever time is left is divided into little pieces. For the majority of us, by the time we're through taking care of everyone else, there isn't much time left for ourselves.

After I gave my daughter a bath and fed her dinner, we went upstairs to get ready for bed. She brushed her teeth twice, and we spent ten minutes looking for her blanket before she finally crawled into bed.

I read her a story, and as I was turning off the light, I reminded her that I was only staying for two minutes. Two minutes is usually much longer, but this helps her understand I have to leave eventually.

As I lay there in the dark next to her, I began to relax. My daughter was tucked in up to her chin, her forehead was touching mine. She smelled of soap and Aqua de Violeta, a Cuban cologne for children. She was sucking her right thumb and with her left hand she played with my hair.

"Do you know how much Mami loves you?" I asked her as I kissed her on the cheek. Pulling her thumb out of her mouth, she answered groggily in Spanish, "*Si Mami, tu me quieres hasta la luna.*" Yes Mami, you love me all the way to the moon.

Someday, she'll understand how a mother's love cannot be measured. She'll understand how it feels to be known not by your given name but known as someone's mom, and what a wonderful feeling that is.

Moments like this shared with my daughter make everything worthwhile. Whether you work outside the home or stay at home with your children, there will always be stressful days—days when you wish life could be simpler.

Particularly on these stressful days, find a moment for some quiet time and more than likely you'll realize how blessed you are and how you wouldn't change places with anyone else.

Spring Break Madness

It is a beautiful day at South Padre Island. The sun is shining and the air is cool. It's not beach weather for us Rio Grande Valley natives, but the beach is filled with kids from all over the United States, many of them swimming in the freezing ocean.

I'm sitting seventeen floors up from all the action. The music from an event being held a block away drifts through the sliding door, and it's hard for me to concentrate on my writing. Every once in awhile when a good song comes on, I get up and walk to the sliding door.

I go out to the balcony and dance with my four-year-old daughter and, for a moment, I remember what it was like to be eighteen again. To be carefree, without worries and responsibilities, when inexperience allows you to believe that nothing can happen to you.

The majority of adults cringe when spring break comes around. They worry about so many young people gathered in one place. They worry about the drinking and everything that comes along with it.

It is true that a lot of wild things occur during spring break. It's scary when you look at the news on TV and watch beer-guzzling contests. But apart from all the wild parties, there is also a very large group of kids just hanging out and having a good time.

As a parent, I worry when my sons are here but the other side of me sees this stage in their life as part of growing up. Unless they see the craziness and the way some people can't handle having fun without losing their heads, they'll never be able to set a level somewhere in between.

The older my sons become, the more I realize that the only way a child learns about life is by experiencing it. As parents, we want to protect them. We share our experiences with them, hoping that they won't make the same mistakes.

We hope some of our words find their way into their brains and become embedded someplace where those words will sound forth whenever they're about to do something wrong.

The scariest words a child can say to a parent is, "Don't worry, Mom, I've got it under control." As adults, we know that life usually isn't under our control. Things happen even when you're being careful. So what do you do? Do you lock up your child until he's eighteen years old? He'll be safe all right, then he'll go off to college, and reality will hit him square in the face.

If you're too strict, your child will do things behind your back. If you're too lenient, you raise a child that has no sense of right and wrong. Finding a balance between the two isn't always easy.

As a mother of a eighteen-year-old college freshman and a sixteen-year-old junior in high school, I've learned to take situations one at a time and deal with them as they come up. We work at keeping the lines of communication open so that our sons can always come to us.

It's 4 o'clock in the afternoon and the beach is packed with bodies. There is nonstop action. The abundance of youthful spirit is everywhere. You can feel it in the air. A sailboat is gliding over the ocean waves. Jet skis are flying in and out of the surf.

I pick up the binocular to see what the shouting and clapping is all about. A dance contest is taking place at the event being held at the Radisson Hotel. Young bikini-clad beauties are on the stage.

Sorority and fraternity flags are flying proudly in the wind surrounded by their members. My sons and their friends are out there somewhere enjoying this gorgeous day.

The young-girl side of me hopes they're having a good time. The mom side of me can't stop worrying and prays that God will watch over them and keep them safe.

MY SON THE SENIOR

The school year has begun, and once again I find myself thinking back on the years my sons attended elementary school. The start of a school year meant taking them shopping for new clothes, buying school supplies, meeting their teachers, and volunteering in their classrooms.

During this stage in my children's life, I spent most of my time doing things that revolved around them. I felt at times that I would go crazy with the endless activities and car pools.

Then they reached middle school and the separation process began. I think it's called middle school not only because your child is halfway into his education but because as parents you find yourself in a transitional stage in your relationship with your child. Your child is going through puberty, and you're going through a scary process as well.

One day your child seems very mature, and you feel great about how well he's doing. The next day he acts like a little boy, and you wonder if he's heard a word you said.

When they reach high school, you find yourself doing less for them. They get their driver's license, and you feel relief at not having to chauffeur them around town. Then the worrying begins. Where are they? What are they doing? Why aren't they home yet?

The first few years in high school, it's a tug of war. Sometimes you let them win; at other times you pull hard on that rope and drag them to your side regardless of how much they complain.

Then your child becomes a senior in high school, and you realize that next year around this time your baby will be off to college and on his own. It would seem that since I've already gone through this once, it would be easier for me, but it's not.

And the thought of my younger son graduating fills me with nostalgia and a yearning for those years when I had them both living under one roof. Those were wonderful years when at bedtime everyone was tucked safely in bed, and I could go to sleep without worrying.

The 6-foot-3-inch young man who now towers over me is the same chubby baby I held in my arms, and it's hard to believe he will be graduating next year. When your child graduates from high school, you don't only miss him; you also miss all that he takes with him.

Many of the friends your children make in elementary school will be the same friends they hang out with when they're older. This group of kids become a part of your family.

My son met his best friend in kindergarten in Mrs. Gonzalez's class at Milam Elementary. I have a picture of them dressed as pilgrims sitting around a table celebrating Thanksgiving. I have pictures of them together during every stage of my son's life.

In middle school they made friends with another boy and since then the three C's have been inseparable. It has been a pleasure watching these boys grow up and having them in my home, feeding them, and listening to their funny stories.

Sometimes when I see these guys standing around my kitchen counter, I am reminded of the little boys I once knew. My memories will always include them, and their presence in our home has always filled our life with the enthusiasm and energy children always bring to a home.

The other night they had dinner with us. I had made *arroz blanco, picadillo* and *frigoles negros*, a very typical

Cuban meal. Not only did they eat all the food on their plate, but I realized they ate it Cuban style. One of them ate the black beans over the rice with the meat on the side. The other preferred just the rice and meat, but he mixed it together before he ate it, like a typical Cuban.

I love these young men! When they leave, weekends will never be the same. I'll miss the noise and the mess and the sound of their footsteps as they come thundering down the stairs and the trail of cologne that they leave as they walk through the den and out the door.

To my three C's and to all the seniors of the year 2000, I wish you a safe and wonderful life. To my son C.S, I love you! Thank you for always sharing your life with us.

You are the True Expert

I think parents should read all the helpful advice they can about child care and raising healthy kids. It's important especially for parents with newborns to feel confident when caring for their baby.

Reading advice from the experts can help you decide what is best for your family. But after reading many books on child care and having children of my own, I have come to the conclusion that raising children is a very personal experience.

After the birth of my oldest son, I read books on the various stages of infancy. My son never turned over, smiled, sat up or crawled when he was supposed to. In fact, he did very little crawling and was walking by the time he was nine months old. When he was twelve months, he climbed out of the crib.

I'll never forget that night. I was sound asleep when I felt a little body crawling over me to snuggle between my husband and me. I panicked. I thought I had left the crib rail down. I got up and checked the crib but everything was secure. I couldn't understand it until a week later.

My son was supposed to be taking a nap, but when I walked past his room I heard loud grunting noises. I found a chubby twelve-month-old boy with one leg in the crib and the other hanging on the side. I ran into the room just before he pushed himself to the floor. By the time our second son was born, nothing could faze me.

Our children used a pacifier and drank milk from a baby bottle until they decided to give them up. Parents often rush their children into doing things they're not ready to do.

Any mother who has more than one child can tell you that every child is different and each has his or her own timetable. Love your child, accept him the way he is, and don't compare him to other children.

My sons were lovable babies who grew into curious toddlers who got into, climbed onto, and jumped off every piece of furniture you can imagine.

During the first four years of their lives, those little boys supported our plumber. Both of them had an unusual curiosity toward watching objects flush down the toilet. They flushed toothbrushes, socks, diapers, and any small object they could find. I survived those first few years by keeping my sense of humor.

Those were hectic and stressful times with very little peace, but they were some of the best times I ever spent with my sons.

My sons are in college now, and if it weren't for my daughter, the house would seem empty. It wasn't easy getting used to them not living at home. It is a completely different stage of motherhood. I've had to learn to let go and accept the fact they have grown up.

I remember rocking the boys to sleep and thinking about what they'd be like when they were older. The amazing thing is that they have grown up without me noticing it.

Embrace parenthood, learn to enjoy the craziness, and rest whenever you can find a little peace. And remember the old saying, "This too shall pass."

SECTION III

LESSONS IN LOVE

Life Partners

"Sole partner, and sole part of all my joys, dearer thyself than all." John Milton

I fell in love with my husband after our second date. Three months after our first date, we were married and then spent a month traveling through Spain.

The longer I am married, the more I am convinced that marriage is largely a matter of luck. It is also a very personal journey. There isn't a right or wrong way. It's finding your own way that is important.

We all have an inner voice buried deep inside us. We should always listen to it, but instead most of the time we choose to ignore it. I know many young women who have walked down that aisle knowing down deep inside they were marrying for the wrong reasons.

I had no doubts about getting married—not even one tiny little one—and that's the only advice I can give any woman trying to make a decision. Listen to your heart!

Life has basic fundamental rules for any kind of relationship to work—similar cultural, educational and religious backgrounds, common goals, and interests. But even all these things don't guarantee a successful marriage.

For a couple to live happily ever after requires many sacrifices. But when you love someone and you're committed to making that person happy, those sacrifices seem small in comparison to all you gain.

Marriage is an opportunity to help the person you love accomplish his or her goals and dreams. In 1987, when I told my husband I had always dreamed of writing, he didn't make fun of me; instead, he went out and purchased a brand new electric typewriter for me.

The first time I sold a children's story, I received a dozen roses with an invitation to a romantic dinner. My husband has taught me about goals, dreams, commitment, and understanding. He has shown me that love is allowing each other the space to follow our dreams.

Marriage has many peaks and valleys, joyous, playful, and sometimes painful. But when we mature in our understanding for each other, our marriage grows stronger. I can no longer imagine myself unmarried. I can no longer tell where he ends and I begin.

I feel my husband lives inside my head. It's uncanny how well we understand each other.

We definitely don't always agree about everything, but we've learned to compromise. And believe me, this isn't an easy feat, especially for two very verbal, strong-willed Cubans! Our sense of humor has helped us not to lose sight of the most important things in life.

I believe there can be only one captain on a ship, but in order to navigate through life and all its rough oceans, we need another person to help us share the storms.

Even today, after all these years, when I see my husband walk into the room, my heart still says "love." He is my *"Cubano."* He is chemistry and magic, and he fills my soul, making my life complete.

FATHER'S CUBAN WAYS

I'm fortunate to have a very loving father whose support I can always count on. Looking through my family album recently, I noticed that in most of my childhood pictures, my father is always standing behind us with his arms around my brother and me. This is a simple gesture that couldn't describe him better.

Growing up, my father was my security blanket. He made me feel safe. I knew that as long as Papi was around, everything was OK.

I remember an energetic father, always working, determined to succeed. A father who would work on Sundays half a day, then take his children to the beach for a couple of hours in the afternoon.

A father who I have never heard complain about being tired or about any difficult situation he's had to face in life. A father who at the age of twenty-six left his family and everything he had in Cuba so that my brother and I could grow up free.

An understanding father who pretended not to notice when I used to crawl into bed between my mother and him on stormy nights.

A courageous father who during the Mariel boat lift rented a shrimper and went to Cuba. He left Key West, Florida, on April 25, 1980, and returned twenty-one days later with his brother, sister-in-law, and their children.

A generous father who over the years has helped friends and family members leave Cuba and begin a new life in the United States.

A loving grandfather who has always been there for his grandchildren and who, by example, has shown them all they can accomplish in life.

My life wouldn't be the same without the wise teachings of my father. He is my friend, my treasure, and my guide. Whenever I listen to an old Cuban ballad or read the verses of Jose Marti, I will always think of my father.

I will continue to learn as much as I can from him so that I can pass on to my children my father's Cuban ways and ideals.

ABUELO SET A GOOD EXAMPLE IN LIFE

My paternal grandfather, Vicente, was a humble, hard-working man. Abuelo Chito was born in 1906 in the Provincia de la Habana. He was second to the oldest and had four brothers and one sister. His father was a farmer. Abuelo and his brothers grew up working in the sugarcane fields. They also grew tomatoes and different *viandas,* (malanga, yuca, yame), vegetables eaten in Cuba. Sometimes when money was tight, Abuelo and his brothers would work on other farms. They would each make twenty-five cents a day. It was enough to buy rice, beans, and eggs.

When Abuelo was twenty-seven, he fell in love and married a young woman who lived on a farm not far from his. When the depression hit and the price of sugar went from eighteen cents a pound to half a cent, Abuelo Chito and Abuela Luisa moved to the city to find work.

Abuelo's first business was on the front porch of the house where my father was born in Güines, Cuba, in 1937. From there, Abuelo moved his business to the Plaza de Mercados, located in the center of the city. He began to sell much more than just fruit and vegetables, and his business became more like a small *bodega*.

In 1952, he moved his family to Havana where he opened Elegante Café on the ground floor of the apartment building where my father grew up. The café was open seven days a week from 6 o'clock in the morning until midnight, except for Sundays when Abuelo would close the café in the afternoon so he could spend time with his family.

The café was out in the open—very typical of Latin American countries and European countries. Patrons would walk up to the bar and drink their *cafecito* and have a quick *pastelito* or Cuban sandwich before they continued on their busy day.

Abuelo also sold Cuban cigars, cigarettes, *batidos de fruta* and soft drinks. My father remembers standing on top of a wooden crate in order to be able to wait on customers. In order to help my grandfather, he would work all day and attend school at night. Sometimes he was so tired he would fall asleep in class.

Those were difficult times, and my father learned at a young age the fundamentals of what's important, such as providing food for the table and keeping a roof over his head and clothes on his back. He grew up watching his father work hard to make ends meet. In his own quiet way, Abuelo taught my father about unselfishness and perseverance.

Men, in general, sometimes have a hard time expressing themselves and showing their children how much they love them. During Abuelo's generation, most of the responsibility for raising the children belonged to the mother.

Today, most fathers are aware of the important role they can play in their children's lives. Regardless of how you were raised or how open you are with your child, the best gift a father can give his child is to live an honorable life.

A good father is someone his family can count on. He is someone who works hard and sets an example not only for his children but also for his grandchildren. He is a man who understands that the value of life is not measured by material possessions, but rather by the quality of a man's life and by the lifetime of memories he leaves behind.

A good father teaches his children to be proud of their past and to love and respect their heritage. He lives his life with honor and love for his family.

Little things often teach us as much as life's epic moments do. These are the ways we all learn to survive. These are the lessons a father carries in his heart and can pass on to his children. To my father and to all the fathers who live their lives setting an example for their families, thank you for all that you do.

Ties That Bind Friends Together

French poet Jean de La Fontaine wrote, "Friendship is the shadow of the evening, which strengthens with the setting sun of life."

Friendship can occur anyplace and at any time. If you're lucky, your parents, your siblings, your spouse, and your children can be lifetime friends. We all need that special best friend, however, the one we turn to for encouragement and support.

I found that special friend in my cousin Mae. By the time she was born, I had already left Cuba with my parents. For years, I knew all about my cousins through letters my mother would receive from her sister.

The first time we met was the summer I turned fifteen. My family and I were on our way to Europe and stopped to visit my aunt and her family who had recently arrived from Cuba via Spain and were living in New Jersey.

My cousin Mae was ten. She was a petite little girl, very bubbly and sweet. I liked her immediately. A few years later when she moved to McAllen with her family, she became the little sister that I had never had.

Because my aunt worked, every day after school my cousin and her sister would come over to my house. We would sit and have our afternoon *merienda* and take turns telling my mother everything we'd done that day. I loved spending time with my younger cousins.

For years my role was that of the older cousin. Whenever Mae needed advice, she'd come to me. As she moved into her early twenties, our conversations were always about her life: college, dating, her move to Los Angeles.

Because I married young, my cousin's life has always been a source of insight into what life was like out there in the singles' world. As she became older, we began to have more things in common, and I was able to talk to her about things we hadn't been able to discuss before.

Our telephone conversations have always been long, and there have been many when one of us has jokingly said, "I hope no one is listening to this!" There are no secrets between us; we have shared everything about our lives with each other.

We have cried together, laughed together, and gotten through tough times because we have had each other to lean on. For quite some time now, our relationship has been on equal ground. I am no longer the older cousin giving advice. We're two grown women who cherish the love and friendship we have found in each other.

The depth of our connection is hard to explain. There have been many times over the years when I'm getting ready to call her, the phone will ring. It will be her. We have the same sense of humor and are so much alike that on Valentine's Day a few years ago, we sent each other the same card. On many occasions, we have bought each other the same books as gifts.

Every milestone my cousin has reached has brought us closer together. Five years ago, she married the man of her dreams. She has found true happiness and can now understand what it's been like for me all these years.

When she became a mother, she took another step towards understanding another part of my life.

She will know now the intensity with which I love my children. She will experience how powerful and frightening a mother's love for her child can be.

Never again will she have the boundless freedom of a childless woman. For the rest of our lives we will not only be cousins and best friends, we will be united by the greatest gift God can give a woman—motherhood.

Follow the Gray Tile Road to Love and Comfort

I live next door to my parents. When I want to visit them, I just walk out a side entrance and follow a gray tile walkway to a gate that connects our homes.

I call it having my own yellow brick road.

My husband has often been asked how he can live next door to his in-laws. He jokingly answers that living next to his mother-in-law is living next to the best Cuban restaurant in town. My children also like having Abuela next door, especially when they don't like the dinner menu at home.

The walkway connecting our homes is my road to comfort, my road to sanity on days when I can't take another stereo blaring or another Barney video. It is the road to sane advice when I wonder if I've made the right parenting decision.

Entering my parent's home is like entering a spa. Tranquility greets me at the door, as well as a kiss and hug from my parents. Once I'm in their home, I'm not a mom or a wife. I become their little girl again. They pamper me, for a change.

Visiting their home helps me refuel. A couple of hours with my parents gives me the boost I need to get going again. The older I get, the more I appreciate them. Their devotion to our family and their views on life has greatly influenced my own.

When we are children, we idolize our parents, but when we become adults we have the opportunity to know them as they really are.

For many, reaching this point is painful because they realize how little emotional support they have received throughout their life. I've learned from my parents that parenthood doesn't end when your children become older, only that your relationship changes. A parent's role is always important in their children's lives regardless of how old they are. My brother and I enjoy my parent's company. We can party with them. We can joke with them and, most importantly, we can go to them anytime with our problems. No two people love and care for us as they do.

When I look back on my childhood, I realize that the relationship I enjoy with my parents is the fruit of all the memories we've shared.

One night when my four-year-old daughter was in bed with a cold and a fever, I was caressing her face and running my fingers through her hair. She placed her cheek on the palm of my hand and fell asleep. This incident reminded me of the times my mother and I used to cuddle just before bedtime. Like my daughter, I would often ask my mother to stay just a little longer. I would place her arm around me and lay my cheek on her forearm. I can still remember how cool her skin felt and the smell of fresh soap mixed in with her perfume.

I used to love sitting with my dad in a dark-brown leather chair he used to have in our old house. We would sit together and watch television. Sometimes I would pretend to fall asleep so that he would carry me to bed. I can still remember the tenderness with which he would gently tuck me in and kiss me good night.

It doesn't matter how old I am, there will always be days when I want to be just Mami's and Papi's little girl. I'm fortunate to be able to walk out my door and down the gray tile road to a home where I'm always greeted with an abundance of love.

My goal is to create the same kind of home for my children. I want to make sure they always have a clear path to their childhood home. I want them to always know they can count on us.

As long as I am on this earth, I will be their mom, and regardless how many grandchildren walk in the door behind them, they will always be my little boys and my little girl.

GRATEFUL FOR GOOD FATHERS

"A great man is he who does not lose his child's heart."[4] Mencius

When my sons were small, I loved watching them play with their father. They both jumped on his back and tried to knock him down. Their laughter was filled with joy and contentment at having their father all to themselves.

Our daughter has brought out the gentler side in my husband. She is a tiny thing compared to her brothers at the same age. She loves to cuddle with her father, and her sweet and affectionate manner melts his heart.

Whenever I watch my husband with our children, I am grateful I married a man who wanted children as much as I did. What a difference this has made in their lives. One of the most urgent domestic challenges facing the world today is the absence of fathers. The traditional two-parent family is a thing of the past.

We learn so much about life by watching the way our father handles his life. He is our guide, our teacher. Throughout a child's life, a father plays many different roles.

When we're in our teens, he becomes an enforcer of rules we don't always agree with. As we get older, we begin to understand him. If we're lucky, he becomes a treasured friend.

Growing up knowing we can count on our father gives us a sense of security. Regardless of how old I am, I will never outgrow a need for my father. No one can put their arms around me and comfort me like he can. I will always be his little girl. And what a wonderful feeling that is.

The Ties That Bind
Brother and Sister

When I was a little girl, my mother would always remind us that cats and dogs fought, but human beings could talk to each other. My little brother was a terror. He rode his bike like a madman, jumped off carports, and loved to play pranks on our neighbors.

Everything I was afraid to do, my brother wouldn't think twice about trying. I stood on the sideline, biting my nails and watching in horror as he performed all sorts of crazy stunts.

His mischievous behavior usually was not directed at me. But I do remember one incident in particular that upset me. I had spent most of my morning bathing my dolls and dressing them in their prettiest outfits. My brother sneaked into my room, grabbed a couple of my dolls and ran outside. He then tied a rope around each of their necks and drove off with my babies bouncing behind his bike.

He couldn't understand why I was so upset. After all, didn't I always want him to play with me? My brother and I were taught to depend on each other at a very young age.

When my family left Cuba in 1963, it was just the four of us. I think those first few years have a lot to do with the kind of relationship I have with my brother as well as with my parents.

We were taught to share everything, especially since there was so little to share at the time. My mother reminded us often that as long as we had each other, we would never be alone.

The older we got, the closer we became. I'm convinced the relationship we have with our siblings has a lot to do with the way our parents raised us. There has never been jealousy or resentment of any kind between my brother and me.

As children, we were taught to be happy for each other and to enjoy the success of one another. They taught me to love my brother, to respect him and to treasure our relationship.

I know that, no matter what I do or what circumstances I find myself in, I can always count on my brother. He is the bond to the most important connection in life—our parents.

I look forward to growing old and sharing my life with my brother. And I hope my relationship with him will set an example for my children, and that they, too, will treasure each other.

True Love Stories Abound

My sixteen-year-old son gave me a great compliment the other day. He came home with a book called *True Love*, written by Robert Fulghum (published by HarperCollins, 1997). Inside the front cover he wrote, "Mom, This book made me think of you. Maybe you can send your story in."

"Tell me a love story. Not one you've read or heard. One you've lived." For several years Fulghum had been asking that of friends and strangers. Mail poured in from across the country, as well as from seven foreign countries. Teenagers in love, elderly folks writing about sacred memories, people from all walks of life described what they considered was true love.

Intrigued by the response he received, he went looking for stories from those who don't like to write. Fulghum made a sign: "Tell me a short love story, and I will buy you coffee and make you famous." He took the sign around Seattle's neighborhood espresso houses, to a couple of bars, and a local neighborhood fair.

The sign always drew a crowd, especially when people understood that all the proceeds from this book were to benefit Habitat for Humanity, an organization founded on the principle that the ultimate grace is found in the simple admonition "Love one another."

At first, Fulghum writes in his book, it wasn't easy getting people to talk about love. Eventually with encouragement, however, they would tell him their story. Several people got standing ovations from the small crowds that would gather around to listen. One love story led to another. "If truth is stranger than fiction," Fulghum wrote, "then true love is even stranger."

My children have grown up listening to me talk about love. They know their mother is mushy, extremely romantic, and someone who cries when watching a sad movie. They know I love roses, candles, and moonlit walks on the beach.

Over the years, they've had to sit and listen while Mom reads beautiful passages from books they wouldn't even consider reading. They know I have a collection of romantic music and that their dad is the love of my life.

I've always made it a point to show them that married people can stay passionately in love with each other. That romance doesn't end just because you have children or you've been married many years.

My parents have been married for over forty-five years. For as long as I can remember, every night they sit next to each other and hold hands while they watch television. My mother walks my dad to the door every time he leaves the house and kisses him good-bye.

My brother and I grew up aware of the love and passion that exists in their marriage. The most wonderful gift they have given us is the example of what can exist between two people. By watching them, we have both always wanted what they have.

My paternal grandfather had a brother who married my maternal grandmother's sister. My parents met when my dad went to live with his uncle in Guantánamo. My mother went to visit her aunt, and my father answered the door.

My mother thought he was the most handsome boy she'd ever met, and my father thought my mother was beautiful. It was like a lightening bolt. In one second their lives changed forever. Forty-five years later, that magic is still in their marriage.

Their marriage is the richest legacy they could bestow on me. I grew up wanting that same magic in my life, and after twenty-seven years of marriage, I can say that I have it. I married someone who appreciates my mushiness and who works just as hard as I do in keeping the magic in our relationship.

Romantic love can exist forever as long as two people maintain a loving and passionate vision of each other. Love stories are unique, and we all have one. Tell your children your love story and by doing so, you'll keep alive the flame that can light up your heart and keep the torch burning.

To My Valentine

When I met my husband, I didn't just fall in love. *I crashed into love*—the kind of love Marc Anthony sings about in his song, "You Sang to Me." The first time this man hugged me, I fit perfectly under his chin, and when he held me, I knew that there was no one else I ever wanted to be with.

When you find love, you feel a sense of gratitude for having met someone unexpectedly who changes the course of your life. I can't imagine living in this world without my husband by my side. Our home is a cocoon that is filled with love and peace. I cherish that peace, that security that comes from being married to someone for so long.

I know that by my side I have a man who is loyal and as committed to our marriage as I am. He is someone I can laugh with and share my dreams. The experiences we have lived through, the good times and the bad times we have had to overcome, have made us one. I know that, as long as we have each other, we can face anything life brings our way.

Valentine's Day can last forever if you really love each other as you should. If you always place each other's love before everything else, love will last and the passion you feel for each other will grow stronger, deeper, and more fulfilling as the years go by.

After so many years together and in the process of raising three children, we have grown to depend on each other. The challenges we have faced as a couple have only added to the love and respect we have for each other. A shared past is powerful. As you grow older, it is sometimes difficult to believe that all that you experienced has really happened.

There are many couples who stay together, but they never totally surrender their hearts. Some continue to play games with each other and are never really honest about how they feel or what they want.

He lives his life. She lives her life. Their daily agendas are filled with meetings and social commitments. The days and months slip by them as they grow farther and farther apart. They don't spend time working on their relationship, and they miss out on the most satisfying experience a couple can ever share. They stay together, but they never live their life as "us." They continue to think of only "me."

When you can share your life with someone, however, everything you do vibrates with warmth and satisfaction.

Love is about looking at each other across a room and feeling that if you don't spend the rest of your life together you will have missed everything. Love is wanting to be with each other regardless of how long you've been married. It's about the intimate secrets you share with each other. Love is like the clouds you cannot touch. Like the flowers after it rains, you are grateful for love on a cold winter night.

When we were newlyweds, I thought that marriage could never get any better. Now I realize that love is like a fire; its ability to warm us is determined by all the experiences we have shared as a couple. Everything we have lived through has added to the flame. Our newlywed years were just sparks that ignited the tinder, but in order to keep that fire burning it takes love, commitment, friendship, and understanding. And then, and only then, can a couple enter the world of the beloved.

Love is one long wonderful dance, and I have been sharing this dance with my husband. On Valentine's Day, couples all over the world will be celebrating this day of love. I, too, shall be celebrating the day with my old flame, my *Cubano*, my lover of twenty-seven years.

EIGHT IS A BEAUTIFUL, INNOCENT EXPERIENCE

My eight-year-old daughter has a unique way of looking at life. I love listening to her talk, and I enjoy the challenge of trying to understand how her little mind works. She is at an age where she's curious about everything.

Last week when we were driving home from ballet, she asked, "If the world is round, then why do we drive everywhere in a straight line?"

My daughter wears her emotions where everyone can see them. She loves with all her heart, and she lets us know how much. She shares hugs and kisses with everyone in the family.

The day before her first day of second grade, she drew a picture with a bright orange sun and a colorful rainbow. Underneath the sun she wrote, "Dear Mom, I love you so much. I am in 2nd grade." She drew big puffy blue clouds and wrote "second grade" underneath them. In between the colors of the rainbow, she wrote, "I love you Mom" and drew hearts. In the right-hand corner, she drew a little girl dressed in pink, with pigtails.

In April, she will be making her First Communion. For the past two years she has been attending Catholic Christian Doctrine classes at Our Lady of Sorrows Church. We have had long conversations about God. The other day on our way home from church, she said, "I think about why God invented us. Why did he? We're just bones under all the skin."

Last week on our way home from CCD, she asked me, "Why do we live?" Before I could say anything, she said, "It's strange the way God invented us. You know, Mom, kids can't listen to God because He never talks to us."

"Yes, He does," I said. "He just doesn't talk to us the way we talk to each other." We had a long discussion about faith and God and the way God is always with us.

She is very curious about how God came up with rainbows and thunderstorms. She thinks He has a great imagination, because He invented the "rain, the spirit and the sun and everything nice."

She wants to know if there are more butterflies than bees, but she knows there are more birds. She knows that when girls go to college, they're more knowledge-able and that boys are from Jupiter and they're more stupider.

Whenever I'm out of town, she leaves long messages on my cell phone. Sometimes I save them so that I can listen to them more than once. A few months ago while I was attending a conference in San Diego, she left me this message:

"Mami, I miss you! I know you are learning new stuff—learn it good. I'm proud of you. I did my home-work all by myself. Well, Tia helped me with the hard part. I miss you! When are you coming home? I'm going to sleep in your room with Papi, so that he doesn't get sad, because you're not home. Do your bestest! I love you with all my heart. It's me, your daughter."

Eight is a great age. It's an age when children believe mom and dad can do no wrong. I hope that as she gets older, she continues to share her rainbows and hearts with us.

BEHOLD THE POWER OF WORDS

Last weekend at the grocery store, I ran into my elementary school teacher, Mrs. Sara Della Croce Meyers. She gave me a warm hug and told me how proud she is of me and how she cuts out all my columns. I don't see her very often, but every time I do, I am reminded of my fifth grade year at Victor Fields Elementary School in McAllen, Texas.

When my sons think about their elementary school years, they are filled with incredibly happy memories. My daughter is having the same kind of experience her brothers did.

My experience was very different from my children's. My family had lived in the United States for just a few years and having just emigrated from Cuba, we were facing very difficult times.

I felt completely lost. My grades were poor and every day I couldn't wait to get home to my mother and the safety of the familiar.

I have always felt that my confusion made my teachers angry and that my lack of participation was considered a form of rebellion. I never felt comfortable enough with any of my teachers to ask for help.

Looking back, I think teachers in the 1960s were not as prepared as they are now to deal with children who spoke Spanish or who came from another country as they are now.

None of my teachers could imagine how difficult it was for me. Everything was new. Because I was the oldest, I would go along to translate for my parents whenever they attended PTA or had a meeting with someone from school.

But everything changed in fifth grade when Mrs. Della Croce became my teacher. I can still picture this very elegant woman walking down the hall of Victor Fields Elementary School. She used to eat yogurt for lunch. I don't know why I remember this—probably because it was the first time I had ever heard of yogurt.

She was loving and kind and extremely patient with me. She tutored me every chance she could. She was the only teacher I had in elementary school who cared about me. She asked to meet my parents and took the time to find out about the family. She invited me to her home, and I remember meeting her daughter.

For the first time in my life, I felt that being a Cuban immigrant and not speaking English was not a bad thing, but that it made me special.

Her sweetness and assurance that I could do the school work helped me want to try harder. She found a way to break down the barrier that was keeping me from learning.

At the end of that school year, Mrs. Della Croce left Victor Fields Elementary. I missed her terribly.

Half way through my sixth grade year, we moved to the north side of town. I was terrified about attending a new school. At Milam Elementary, the school secretary walked me to my classroom and held the door open for me. I took one step into the room, and standing right there, in front of the class, was Mrs. Della Croce.

Running into her at the grocery store thirty-two years later and hearing her say she is proud of me means more to me than she can imagine.

Words are powerful and can have an incredible impact on our lives. Author Maya Angelou once wrote, "I'm convinced that the negative has power—and if you allow it to perch in your house, in your mind, in your life, it can take you over."

Buried in my heart are memories of a little girl who shed many tears of loneliness and frustration.

We often are quick to label children as difficult, loners, shy, uncooperative, when what we should be doing is figuring out a way to reach out to them.

Words have the power to destroy, to heal, and to encourage others. I feel blessed that, at a difficult time in my life, a teacher who used her words with love and care allowed one very confused little Cuban girl to find her way.

LOVE AND ROMANCE GO HAND IN HAND

Of all the gifts God has given us, love enables us to find meaning in life. It's amazing how something that is invisible can transform your life.

Love makes you smile; or it can break your heart. Love can give you goose bumps and hot flashes. But most importantly, without love, we would not be here.

Love tears down the walls we so often build around ourselves. How blessed we are when we meet that certain someone who we allow into the door of our hearts.

For some people, relationships are scary and risky. In order for a relationship to work, we have to open up to allow our partner to know the real person.

I read once that a relationship is like a path of initiation that takes us through a journey with many tests and trials.

A writer starting to work on a story needs to have an idea of what it is he is going to say. An artist has to have a vision in mind of what it is he wants to create.

A relationship works very much in the same way. In order for a relationship to work, we have to understand what it is we want. You have to have a vision of where you want it to go.

Love just happens. It can happen in a second. But relationships are a growing process, and if you and your partner lose each other along the way, the relationship stops moving forward. It gets stuck.

That is where romance comes in and why it can keep your relationship exciting. The longer I'm married, the more I believe that romance is an important part of a relationship.

When a couple begins to date, life revolves around the romance. Every time you hear a song on the radio, you think of him. You can't wait until you see him again. You make time for each other, over everything else.

Children, work, and life can make havoc of a relationship if the couple doesn't stay focused on each other. Having real moments of intimacy, keeping romance alive, and taking care of each other will help a relationship get through difficult times.

You can be with a person physically, but emotionally be on another planet. Relationships are about connecting on a deeper level. A happy relationship has nothing to do with a piece of paper that proves you are married. A relationship is all about how you love and respect your partner. It's about the place you give your partner and the choices you make as a couple.

Go out to dinner, drive to the beach for the day, light candles, sit in front of a fireplace—do all those romantic things you used to do. Rekindle the love and passion everyone deserves to have in life.

Essence

Searching through a box
I found the small bottle
Of Calendre you gave me in 1977,
The fragile fragrance brought back memories
Of the summer we fell in love.

I closed it carefully
so as not to lose
the little that remains
Of the sweet-scented perfume.

One small drop
and fragrant memories fill my heart
with the essence of our love.

I love you! J.S.

Section IV

The Cuban in Me

Los Cubanos de Texas—
THE CUBANS FROM TEXAS

The first time I visited Miami was in 1968. We drove to Florida in my father's 1966 Chevrolet Impala. I remember as if it were yesterday. We left McAllen early in the morning. It was still dark out, and the sky was filled with stars as my brother and I lay in the backseat with pillows and blankets. Visiting Miami opened up a whole new world for me; up to that point in my life, I wasn't sure what it meant to be Cuban.

Vivid images come to my mind whenever I think of that trip. The smell of Cuban expresso brewing the first time I visited a Cuban café, and the way the Cuban waitress looked behind the counter as she laughed and joked with the patrons. The taste of my first Cuban sandwich—slices of pork, ham and swiss cheese between a delicious bread (similar to French bread)—as we sat at the Latin American cafeteria on Coral Way.

I remember the sound of salsa music blaring from the speakers in a record shop, and the way the owner looked dancing behind the counter. I remember the *chispa* so typical of the Cuban people, and the way they talk with their hands. There was the sight of Cuban men wearing white guayaberas, standing in front of a café smoking their Cuban cigars and talking about politics.

Like my parents, my husband and I want our children to be exposed to their Cuban roots. Like so many Cubans who live outside Miami, we have made it a point to take our children there as often as possible.

Every year a few days after Christmas, my family packs their bags, and we fly to Miami for a week. It's a yearly pilgrimage to Cubanism and to a way of life I want our children to experience.

When we arrive, Rigoberto, the owner of a car rental agency, is waiting for us at the airport with a van. Before we head to our apartment, we always stop at Versailles Restaurant on 8th street. The minute we walk in, Ernesto, the maitre d' who has worked there for years, sees us and greets us like old friends. "*Llegaron los Cubanos de Texas*," he'll say to nobody in particular. He ushers us to a table as he tells us the latest Cuban joke circulating in Miami.

Before we look at the menu, we order *mariquitas*, banana chips, and *yucca frita*, fried yucca sliced like french fries. Some of us order a *batido de mamey*, a delicious fruit shake. The rest of the group drinks *Materva*, a Cuban soft drink.

Lunch is a feast. Everyone orders something different, *arroz con pollo al imperial*, chicken and rice; *vaca frita*, a type of shredded beef; *frijoles negros, arroz blanco y maduros*, black beans, white rice and sliced ripe plantains; and *viste de palomilla con congri*, a palomilla steak with black bean rice.

Visiting Miami gives my children the opportunity to spend time with their *Abuelos*. They have the opportunity to listen to Abuelo reminisce about Cuba and to catch a glimpse of what life in Cuba was like. We visit Cuban museums and bookstores. We go to see Cuban plays, and we spend a week eating delicious Cuban food.

This past New Year's Eve when we were all dancing a conga, I looked around the room and saw my husband, my parents, and my children. I thought, "This is what it's all about, and what I want my children to remember."

My family is a little bit Cuban and a little bit American. It's *arroz con pollo* and hamburgers. It's salsa and rock and roll. I want my children to hold on to all the good things about our Cuban heritage and incorporate them into their American life. We are a combination of both, and without one or the other, life would not be complete.

TURKEY DAY

I will always remember my first Thanksgiving celebration. We had come from Cuba via Spain only months before and it was, financially and emotionally, the worst year our family ever has had to face.

I had just started kindergarten, and I was learning English. Our class was studying history about the Pilgrims, who had come on the Mayflower, and about the Indians. My teacher described the feast they had shared and how they had eaten turkey and fresh vegetables grown by the Indians.

A turkey! That caught my attention. That night I announced to my parents that Turkey Day was only a week away and that my teacher had said everyone had to eat turkey on that day.

"Why?" asked my mother.

"Because," I said smartly, "that's how it is done in America."

At the time, my father was working twelve hours a day. He was barely making ends meet. A turkey was a luxury we could not afford. But my father found a way, and that Thanksgiving we celebrated our first Cuban-American Thanksgiving dinner. It doesn't matter that I didn't understand the significance then, only that it was the first step taken toward something very American.

It's been forty years since our first Thanksgiving Day celebration. A lot has changed since then. The family fabric business has prospered, and my father no longer has to worry about not having enough money. The holidays are no longer spent alone, but with a house full of family. Yet for us, as for many Cubans in the United States, there always is a shadow of sadness lurking during the holiday season as we think of those we know and love who still suffer in a Communist Cuba.

Whenever I think back on that first Thanksgiving Day, I'm always touched by the effort and sacrifice my parents put forth to make it such a special day for us. As a child, I never realized how tough things were and how lonely and frightening those first few years must have been for them. Both my parents were in their mid-twenties with two small children to care for. They were in a country where they knew no one and did not speak the language. Yet my parents never complained, and I remember a childhood filled with warmth and happiness.

Over the years, Thanksgiving has become one of my favorite holidays. As a Cuban-American I have a lot to be thankful for. Like the Pilgrims, I also came in a ship, but instead of finding Indians in our new home we found a wonderful group of people from all parts of the world. We found a land of freedom, a land of hope, and a place to fulfill our dreams.

I am married now to a Cuban, and with our children we share in a special Thanksgiving dinner, Cuban style. On Thanksgiving Day we arrive at my parents' home around noon. The men sit and watch football games.

Like most Americans, we have a turkey with all the trimmings. But I have yet to meet a Cuban who can give up his white rice, black bean soup, and delicious fried bananas.

One thing I always will be thankful for is my dad buying that first turkey. That was the first step taken toward the beginning of a new life. This Thanksgiving, I will thank my dad for giving me the opportunity to enjoy the best of two cultures.

And when my family is gathered around the dinner table, I will remind them of something I read by Jeremy Taylor: "The private and personal blessings we enjoy, the blessings of immunity, safeguard, liberty, and integrity, deserve the thanksgiving of a whole life."[5]

TOUGH TIMES AREN'T ALWAYS BAD TIMES

As the wife of a businessman, I know how difficult it is for residents of the Rio Grande Valley whenever Mexico faces a peso devaluation. But as a Cuban immigrant, I know that no matter how difficult the situation, my family will never be worse off than when we came to this country.

When we left Cuba in 1963, all our belongings were taken from us. In Havana, before boarding the plane, soldiers took all of our clothing except one change of clothes per person. They took my parents' wedding rings and all of my father's money. They even took my brother's baby bottle. The soldiers tore up family pictures and tossed them in the trash. That was their way of punishing us for leaving.

I try to imagine how my parents felt as they were sitting on the plane headed toward Madrid with two small children and no money. In Spain, a Cuban refugee organization helped us find a place to stay and gave us food and clothing. Everyone, regardless of what they'd had in Cuba, was in the same situation.

My father immediately went to work doing odd jobs. We tease him about his role as an extra in the movie *The Fall of the Roman Empire*. We have pictures of him dressed in a robe and sandals, standing next to other Cubans he met while filming the movie.

When my father raised some money, he put my mother, brother and me on a train to Barcelona. We lived with my mother's family for six months. My father didn't join us until he had earned enough to pay for our tickets to the United States. We left Spain on September 5, 1963, and arrived in New York eleven days later on a ship called the *Covadonga*.

In Cuba we had led a comfortable life. But having to start over meant giving up everything. My parents were never bitter about suddenly being poor. Material deprivations were not important. What mattered was that we had our freedom, and our family was together.

When we moved to McAllen, my father went to work in the family-owned fabric store and my mother stayed home. For years my parents took no vacations. Mother bought only what we needed. She learned to sew and made all of our clothing. Every penny was saved so we would never have to borrow money.

My father's drive and discipline finally paid off. Forty years later, he is a successful businessman. My parents accomplished the American dream. Wanting to better ourselves is a normal instinct, but we need to plan for things realistically. We need to put our priorities in order and take things one step at a time.

Most successful people will tell you they never dreamed of reaching as far as they did. They started out slowly, reaching one goal at a time, concentrating on their task enthusiastically.

Material things can come and go, as many Cuban families know from experience. The most important things have nothing to do with having money or costly belongings. But they have everything to do with the way you deal with problems and live your life.

Having faith in God, loving your family, and the memories you carry in your heart—these are the things that no one can ever take from you.

Salsa Lessons

When I was growing up, Saturday was cleaning day. Protest did no good; so reluctantly my brother and I would drag our feet into the kitchen where my mother would tell us what we had to do.

My mother did all the heavy cleaning. We usually had something simple to do. I would dust all the furniture and make the beds. My brother would vacuum and throw out the trash.

Just before we got started, mother, who has always had a knack for making even the most mundane chore fun, would turn on the record player. It didn't matter how tired we were. Once the music came on, we would come alive. With salsa blaring from the record player, cleaning somehow became easier.

My mother would dance with the broom, the mop or a pillow; everything became a dancing partner. My brother and I would laugh, and eventually we would all end up dancing. The beat of the bongo drums in salsa music has a way of crawling into your soul, and once you're hooked there is no turning back.

I have always loved music and was eager to learn to dance. Mami began teaching me steps. She instructed me how to keep my upper body steady while swaying my hips and moving my feet to the beat.

My mother knew most of the words to the songs, and she would sing while twirling me around the room. We would do conga lines and dance in and out of all the rooms in our little house.

Every time a good song came on, we would drop what we were doing and begin dancing. It wasn't uncommon for my dad to come home for lunch and find his wife and children dancing and the housecleaning still not done.

At first, my brother wasn't too enthusiastic about learning to dance. He would roll his eyes, pretend he wasn't interested, but my Mom never got discouraged. She'd ignore his sulking and entice him into joining us.

As he became older and realized that girls like boys who can dance, his interest in learning grew. Although salsa is very different from other forms of dancing, it gave us the flexibility to pick up steps to the music of our generation.

The habit of putting on music whenever I have to do chores at home has never left me. Anytime I have to get busy, you'll hear salsa blaring from the speakers installed all over my house.

I also dance with sofa cushions and imaginary partners while my children laugh at their nutty mom. I taught my sons how to dance this way and now my nine-year-old daughter and I enjoy many dance sessions.

Thinking back on those Saturday mornings, I realize that we were learning more than just how to dance. We learned that life isn't always easy or fun, but we have the ability to make the most out of every situation. The important thing is the attitude we choose to have when dealing with the circumstances we find ourselves in.

Music kept my mother sane those first few years in the United States. It helped her deal with her sadness. It helped her forget how broke we were and how uncertain the future was. Sometimes I'm sure the music took her back to Guantánamo, to the carnivals and a carefree time in her life. A time when Cuba was really Cuba, and Cubans were living life as they should.

Salsa reminds me of my Caribbean roots. The words to the songs talk of the island where I was born. It helps me stay connected to a place and a way of life I have always been curious to know. When I'm dancing salsa, the beat of the drums beat steadily with my heart, and for a moment this Cuban girl is back in Guantánamo.

La Prima de Amerika

Whenever I visit my cousins in Barcelona, they introduce me as *la prima de Amerika*. They say this with pride, as if having a cousin in America gets them a little closer to the country most of them have always dreamed of visiting.

America—everyone wants to visit or eventually live in this great nation. Immigrants are constantly seeking the American dream. America is the land of liberty—the land of endless opportunity. There is no nation on earth that has provided security or shouldered the responsibility of so many as our nation has.

A message written on the base of the Statue of Liberty says: "Give me your tired, your poor, Your huddled masses yearning to breathe free..." Lady Liberty has kept her promise to my Cuban family and to millions of immigrants.

When the French built the Statue of Liberty, it stood only for an ideal. I'm sure the French never imagined that their gift would become the symbol for all the waves of immigrants.

As a Cuban-American, I don't take my freedom for granted. The Statue of Liberty is not just a symbol to me; it represents American values and everything I love about this country.

Harry Ward Beecher wrote, "The real democratic American idea is, not that every man shall be on a level with every other, but that every one shall have liberty, without hindrance, to be what God made him."[6]

As immigrants, we should never expect America to give us anything other than freedom and the opportunity to work. We should not abuse its generosity. Instead, we should strive to better ourselves so we also can contribute to this nation. We should all share concern for this nation's future. We must never forget the ethics and standards that make our country great.

This Fourth of July, once again my family is experiencing the wonder of this great nation. After thirty-five years of suffering in Castro's Communist regimen, my uncle and his family have finally been allowed to leave Cuba.

For my mother, it is a lifetime dream come true. Since my parents moved to McAllen in 1963, she has been bringing her family to the Rio Grande Valley one by one. Her sisters were all reunited in 1980 when my youngest aunt arrived during the Mariel boat lift. My grandmother arrived soon after and was granted the satisfaction of spending her last few years with her daughters.

I had hoped my grandmother would live long enough to see her son finally free. But somehow I know that Abuela and Abuelo are watching from up above and maybe even had something to do with this wonderful reunion. We have been blessed. I have finally met not only my cousins, who were all born after I had left Cuba, but also their husbands and children.

My family is finally free! Free to worship in the church of their choice. Free to read and write and say whatever they feel. Free to work and choose whatever kind of life they want. They are finally freed from all the heavy chains of a Communist country.

I will never again walk into the grocery store and wonder if my family has enough to eat. I will never again have to censor a letter for fear of saying something that could hurt them. Holidays can finally be celebrated with all the joy they were intended to bring.

This Fourth of July, firecrackers will be heard popping and snapping in the streets of American towns.

Americans everywhere will be celebrating this nation's birthday. In McAllen, Texas, thirty-five Cuban-Americans and Cuban immigrants also will be celebrating. Our picnic will be a mixture of young and old, Cuban and American traditions. Together we will celebrate the values of the Statue of Liberty and the American flag, with warmth and love for this country.

Thank you, America, for the opportunities you have given my family. We will never forget how precious our freedom is, and I will always remind my children how lucky they are to have been born Americans.

Have a happy Fourth of July!

From, *la prima de Amerika*.

The Year a Flower Bloomed

I was in second grade and felt like a creature from another planet. It had been three years since my family and I had emigrated to the United States from Cuba. The older I got, the more out of place I felt.

My spelling and grammar were not improving, and the English language and I were at war. I hated having to learn English. It made me uneasy, and it confused me. Every day I would sit in class and wish the day would go by quickly so that I could go home.

After school I would rush into my mother's arms and into the comfort of my Spanish language. My parents did everything they could to help me, but they finally decided to hire Mr. Bloom.

"What a name," I thought the first day we met. Bloom—isn't that what flowers do in spring? Mr. Bloom was a retired teacher who tutored children for extra income. He was a tall, heavily-set man in his sixties with a sunny disposition and kind gray eyes.

From the start, I made every attempt to dislike him. During my lesson I would yawn, look out the window or scribble on a piece of paper. I wanted him to understand that I was not interested in learning English.

At the end of every lesson Mr. Bloom would read me a story. I tried not to listen but eventually realized I could understand almost every single word he said. He always read funny stories that made me laugh, and before long I began to look forward to our afternoons.

As we became friends, I began to trust him and, like a flower in a garden that blooms from the warmth of the sun, I let Mr. Bloom into my life. Slowly, without realizing it, I began to absorb that dreaded English language.

My grades improved, my attitude changed toward school, and for the first time I began to enjoy all the wonderful things that took place around me. I no longer felt English had been invented to torture me, and I accepted it as part of my new American life.

A few years later I would watch my first Charlie Brown cartoon. I remember thinking how much his teacher's voice resembled the way I heard the English language those first few years.

One day as a treat for bringing home a good report card, Mr. Bloom invited me to dinner. I wish I could remember where we ate, but all I can remember is reading the menu and trying to decide what it was I wanted to eat. After a delicious dinner, the waiter brought the dessert cart. My mouth watered at the sight of a strawberry pie topped with whipped cream.

I will never forget that day, sitting with my new friend and savoring my strawberry pie. That day I decided I liked to speak English, especially if it meant I could say, "Mr. Bloom, may I please have another piece of strawberry pie with whipped cream on top?"

Going Home Again

"Home is where the heart is." We've heard this so many times, but it usually means more to us during the holidays. For most of us, returning to our parents' home is comforting. It brings back memories and gives back to us a bit of our childhood.

When my family emigrated from Cuba, we lived in a one-bedroom apartment on the corner of Chicago Avenue and 12th Street in downtown McAllen. The old McAllen Memorial Football Stadium used to be right across the street.

While living there, we met a doctor and his wife who had an office down the block from us. They were curious about us since we were the first Cubans they had ever met. The couple owned a house behind the apartment. When it became vacant, they offered it to my parents for the same amount of money we were paying in the one-room apartment. Their kindness is something my family has never forgotten.

The old house had a front porch, a living room, three small bedrooms, one bathroom, and a tiny kitchen. A few days before moving into our new house in September 1964, my father received a $1000 bonus check at work. My parents took that money to Azteca Furniture Store on 17th Street and Beaumont, and with $900 they furnished the whole house.

They bought a beige vinyl sofa and love seat, a cocktail table and two end tables to match, a dining room table with four chairs, a bedroom set for their room, and two twin beds, one for my brother and one for me. Shopping for furniture back then wasn't very much fun, especially since my parents had to buy what they could afford, not what they liked.

As my parents were leaving the furniture store, the salesman came running after them with two of the most horrendous looking lamps my mother had ever seen. Mother thought he wanted to sell her the lamps. But when the salesman told her they were a gift from the store, she took them happily. The lamps were huge with tangerine striped bases, and they graced our living room for many years.

Every opportunity my parents had they worked at fixing up the old house. When they decided the house needed a fresh coat of paint, my father went to the hardware store. Surprised by how expensive paint was, he bought what was on sale. A few hours later he came home with gallons of green paint. Green—as in bright green, grass green, very green! From that day on, our house became "*la casita verda*" and even today we always refer to it that way.

"*La casita verde*" became the first property my father owned in the United States. We lived in that house for only five years, but it has always seemed longer. A few years ago when my father was going to build on the property, he sold the little house.

My parents and I took my sons through it one last time. As I walked through the dusty rooms taking pictures, I could hear the walls whispering to me, reminding me of childhood memories I will never forget. This little house was where my parents talked about all their hopes and dreams, where four Cuban immigrants learned to become a little bit more American. I have always felt pride in having lived in this old house.

The material things we accumulate in life are a bonus. They make life better but all these things are replaceable. It doesn't matter how big or small your home is. What is important is who lives inside.

A house generous with love, filled with family ready to welcome you home is the only thing that really matters.

Family Ties Bind Generations

My mother has often described to me a photograph that hung in my grandparents' dining room in Cuba. The picture of my grandfather, his parents, and brothers was taken during one of my grandfather's last trips to Spain.

Abuelo was a Spaniard who emigrated to Cuba with a younger brother during the early 1900s. His first few years in Cuba were difficult, but Abuelo worked hard and eventually became a successful rancher in Guantánamo.

When he was forty-two, he fell in love with my twenty-six-year-old grandmother. She was the daughter of a rancher and Spaniard with whom my grandfather did business. They married in 1935 and had five children. Family was very important to my grandfather, and he was sad to be living so far away from his own family. He often spoke about the house where he was born and the vineyards surrounding the grounds.

He wrote to his family often, and my mother grew up hearing stories about life in Spain. Even though Abuelo lived most of his adult life in Cuba, he never gave up his Spanish citizenship. He was very proud of being a Spaniard, of being Catalan.

Abuelo was born in a small village in the Province of Cataluña. Pla de Penedes is about a two-hour drive from Barcelona. The Spaniards in this area speak Catalan, a language very similar to French. When we left Cuba in 1963, we lived in Spain with my mother's family for six months.

The day we arrived we were greeted by a house full of relatives. There were many tears of joy and the customary kiss on both cheeks. For generations, the Boada family business has been to produce Cava (Champagne). The labels on the bottle have my mother's maiden name.

My brother and I loved living there and playing with our cousins, who were the same age we were. I can still remember our afternoon snacks of a slice of bread (similar to French bread) dipped in red wine and sprinkled with sugar. By the time we left Spain, my brother and I could speak a few words of Catalan. A few years ago on one of my trips, I bought a dictionary in Catalan with Spanish translations.

My relatives sometimes forget my mother and I don't speak Catalan and write us only in that language. Every time I visit this magical place is like never having left it: the house, the cellars underneath it, and the bottles of Cava stacked neatly in rows echo generations of Boadas.

I love to stand in the doorway of the house and look out towards the vineyards. It always reminds me of my grandfather. I imagine Abuelo standing in the same doorway and feeling the same joy I do every time I visit this beautiful country. I'm grateful to him for preserving family ties. His love for his family has given me the opportunity to share my Spanish roots with my children.

When my uncle came from Cuba last summer, in the bottom of his suitcase he brought the photograph of my grandfather and his family. There is nothing more important in life than *la familia*. Strong family ties go on for generations and bless our lives with love and the spirit of our Abuelos.

The Guava Tree

A few years ago, a friend of mine gave me a guava tree she brought on the plane in a small pot from Miami. This tree is special not only because it bears a delicious fruit but because it comes from a Cuban seed. This guava tree was born on Cuban soil just as I was.

I pampered this seven-inch tree for almost a year while our house was being built.

After we moved into our new house on September of 1991, I planted the tree in our yard. For five years, I watched this small tree grow.

I gave it vitamins and fertilized it. In the winter, I would cover it making sure the freeze wouldn't kill it. Another summer would come and go and still there would be no sign of its fruit.

Cuban guava experts and family members would inspect it, nod their heads and tell me to forget it. I refused to give up. This seed had come a long way, and I was determined it would grow on American soil.

Last summer as I was walking past my tree I noticed it had a strong flowery scent. Inspecting it closer, I saw many small white flowers, the first sign that my tree would bear fruit. Finally in August of last year my tree gave me guavas.

For those who don't know what a guava is, let me share some information about one of my favorite fruits. A guava is a pale green aromatic fruit grown in tropical and subtropical areas such as Florida, Cuba, and Hawaii. It is oval shaped with a thick skin and ranges in size from two to four inches, has pink or yellow flesh, and small seeds that are edible.

There are different varieties of guavas. The Mexican variety is egg size and the fruit is pink or white in the center. The Cattley guava is small, and its center is yellow or dark red. The most common is the plum-size guava with pink centers that grows in Florida.

Guavas grow on shrubs and small trees of the myrtle family. It has a strong flowery scent and smooth skin. You can eat the fruit when it's ripe or make delicious desserts with it.

Guava shells (*casco de guavas*) are a favorite Cuban dessert. The guavas are peeled, sliced in half, and the seeds are removed and saved to make guava jelly. The fruit is boiled with cinnamon sticks and brown sugar until tender. The guava shells are then served over slices of cream cheese. The combination of the smooth cream cheese is delicious against the piquant flavors of the guava shells.

Another favorite way to eat guavas is in a paste form. A preserve is made by boiling the pulp until it becomes a solid mass that can be sliced. It is used in pastries and desserts or eaten over a piece of cheese.

As a child, my father would buy slices of guava paste and cheese for two cents in the streets of Havana. A favorite *merienda* for Cuban children is *pan con timba*. Guava paste is sliced, then placed over Cuban bread.

Around the country in Hispanic markets, guavas are sold canned in shell form (*casco de guava*) or the jelly form (*mermelada de guava*). In paste form, it comes in 13-ounce to 18-ounce paste loaves (*cajeta de guayaba*).

Every afternoon, my daughter and I go outside and bring in a basket of guavas. She has learned how to distinguish a ripe guava from the rest. There is nothing like picking fresh fruit from a tree you've planted.

Being able to share this small part of my heritage with my children is important to me. Every time I eat a guava, I am ingesting a bit of Cuban fruit. Whenever the fruit is boiling on the stove, the fragrant smell flows through my house. This small fruit with its unique taste always reminds me of who I am and where I'm from.

Someday I'll be able to go to Cuba and pick guavas from my Abuelo's trees. But, until then, having a piece of Cuba in my back yard is the next best thing.

TREASURES IN THE ATTIC

One of the things I regret most about leaving Cuba is having left behind family keepsakes. A few weeks before my family left the country, soldiers came to our house and took inventory of all our belongings.

Everything my parents owned was confiscated by the government, except for a few items my father had sneaked out of the house months before. My mother packed a box with some of our baby pictures, her wedding album, and a few other items she couldn't bear to part with. She left them at my grandparent's home.

The day we left Cuba, mother packed a few pictures in her luggage hoping she might be able to get them past the soldiers. Those pictures were torn and thrown in the trash in front of us by Cuban soldiers just before we boarded the plane for Spain.

Eventually, all my aunts left Cuba and my Abuelo's house became a storage for all the sentimental things no one could part with. When my grandmother left Cuba, the Cuban government confiscated her house.

Having no one in Cuba with whom to leave those items, Abuela and my aunt made a bonfire in the backyard and burned everything. As they stood watching all the family memories go up in flames, Abuela said they both cried.

I'm always cleaning out my closets and giving things away. However, neatly packed and labeled in large storage boxes are items that I will never part with. These things have no value to anyone except to me because they remind me of special moments in my life.

I can't imagine walking out of my house and leaving behind all the sentimental items I've saved throughout the years. The outfit I wore when I left Cuba and the doll I carried that day. A small wooden treasure box my father brought me from his first business trip to New York. These things are precious to me.

The baby-doll clothing my mother made for me one Christmas. The first gift my brother bought me with his own money, a windup alarm clock that plays the theme to *Love Story*.

Hanging in a bag in the corner of my closet is the outfit I wore on my first date with my husband. I also have a miniature bottle of Calandre perfume he gave me on our second date. The fragrance that lingers in the empty bottle always reminds me of the summer we fell in love.

In a keepsake box is my wedding dress, and hanging on my bedroom wall in a shadow box is a silk replica of my wedding bouquet. On our honeymoon, while walking on the beach in Torremolinos, Spain, my husband found a perfectly round rock. I keep this small rock in the same box with every card my husband has ever sent me.

In our attic is a box filled with scrapbooks from my high school years and a box filled with items from my husband's college and bachelor years.

If I could have rummaged through my grandparent's attic, I would have looked for the old phonograph they had out at the ranch—the one Abuelo would crank up every night after dinner and then dance to the music with my mother and her sisters. I would search for pictures of my mother as a little girl, which I've never seen.

I would look for items that belonged to my grandparents like the safari helmet Abuelo always wore out on the ranch or the Spanish fan my grandmother coquettishly used to fan herself on warm afternoons while sitting in a rocking chair on the verandah.

For many Cuban families who had to leave everything behind in Cuba, it is as though part of their life never took place. Things from our past are like pieces of a chain that link one generation with another. They are a glimpse of the different times we've lived and describe a bit of the person we were during that stage. Family mementos connect you to those you loved and who have passed on.

Someday when I'm babysitting my grandchildren, I'll take them up to the attic and show them a box filled with baby clothing and toys that belonged to their parents. I'll let my granddaughters dress up in my old dresses, and we'll laugh at some of the things I wore. I'll help them discover boxes of accumulated mountains of love and share with them a lifetime of treasures.

Try Giving a Simple Gift: Love

I have been blessed with wonderful parents and have learned a lot from watching them deal with the problems they've faced as Cuban immigrants. During my childhood I received many gifts of love, but one in particular was a very special Christmas I will never forget.

I was nine years old and, like most children, I didn't realize what my parents were going through. The only thing on my mind was making sure Santa understood my Christmas list. I wanted a kitchen set with a stove top, oven, a sink, and a refrigerator. Every time I'd walk past the toy store, I would show my mother which one it was.

I remember my mother commenting on how expensive it was, and I assured her that Santa could afford it. I'd dream about playing in my kitchen, cooking lunch for my dolls, and having tea parties with my neighbors.

On Christmas Eve I went to bed early, anxiously awaiting Santa's arrival. My brother and I left a glass of milk and cookies for Santa and a bowl of grass for the reindeer.

The first thing I saw the next morning is something I will never forget. Sitting on top of my dresser wearing new clothes were the only four dolls I owned. The baby doll I had brought from Cuba had on a new bonnet with a light blue flannel top and a matching diaper. "Giggles" was wearing a new mini-dress and a bow to match. My two big dolls had on party dresses made of satin and chiffon. One was dressed in pink, the other in pastel blue with beautiful flower hair ornaments.

I was so excited I forgot all about my kitchen set, and I ran to tell my parents what Santa had done. I can never think about that Christmas without getting tears in my eyes. I think about the hours my mother spent sewing, her hands lovingly dressing my dolls.

As parents we always want the best for our children. We want to give them all we didn't have and more. But sometimes we forget what is really important. Some parents think giving their children expensive gifts can make up for the time they don't spend at home, when in reality all our children need is our love and attention.

The very first book my father bought me was *The Little Prince*. From this book I'd like to share these words with you:

"It is only with the heart that one can see rightly: what is essential is invisible to the eye."

If parents would only realize that the search for the perfect gift is simple: it lies within our hearts. The most important gift we can give our children is a lifetime of happy memories.

LITTLE THINGS DESERVE THANKS

"Life is such a challenge, such a joy to live when it is appreciated. If we could only realize who gave us life, we would understand even more why He intended us to appreciate and love all that is about us."[7] Joyce Hifler

As a Cuban-American, I live with the constant reminder of how blessed I am. "Life is what we make it" is such a simple statement. Yet, if we never understand this, happiness will always elude us.

My family's recent arrival from Cuba has given us all the opportunity to enjoy the gratitude of twelve individuals who have lived without the simplest of life's pleasures. Watching the faces of my nieces and nephew when I took them trick-or-treating this past Halloween is something I will never forget. They couldn't understand why strangers would be so generous and fill their bags with candy.

I was touched by their reaction when my neighbor asked them to take all the candy they wanted. Each of them chose only one piece of candy. My neighbor had to insist before they took more.

These children were born in a country filled with hunger and sorrow, where worrying about your next meal is the most important thing on everyone's mind. Paper towels, napkins, plastic milk containers, and glass jars are luxuries most don't possess.

When my cousins go to the stores, they marvel at the different colored clothing. They are in awe of the attractive packaging on the shelves. My family is enjoying the enthusiasm of the American people. In no other country are people so ready to celebrate life.

Halloween, Thanksgiving, Hanukkah, Christmas, New Year's, Super Bowl, Valentine's Day, Easter—it's an endless list of occasions to celebrate. In a Communist country there is nothing to look forward to—only a bleak existence. People become angry and bitter. Generosity, friendship, and loyalty are not a way of life.

Most of us are blessed with many things that fill our lives with pleasure, and yet we seldom take the time to enjoy them. We take for granted the beauty of our city; the landscaped homes, banks and public buildings, and the wonderful schools our children attend.

We take for granted the generosity of different organizations that raise money for the needy and the hundreds of volunteers who give their time to help others. On the first official Thanksgiving Day in 1789, an Army surgeon near Valley Forge said, "Mankind is never truly thankful for the benefits of life until they have experienced the want of them."

This Thanksgiving, look around your home and be thankful for the little things God has provided your family. Stop to appreciate the sound of your children's laughter, the beauty of your garden, the bounty on your dinner table.

Let the spirit of the Thanksgiving holiday enter your life; let it promote friendship, love, and unity.

APPRECIATING THE OLDER GENERATION

When I was growing up, I didn't have the opportunity to spend time with my *abuelos*, and it is something I have always regretted. In 1980 when my paternal grandparents arrived from Cuba, I was filled with questions about my father's youth. Every once in a while we talked about the past, but most of the time they didn't remember or the memories were too painful to talk about.

The same thing happened with my maternal grandmother when she arrived a year later. Whenever she talked about her life in Cuba, she began to cry. She would think about my grandfather, who died a few years after we had emigrated to the United States, and I would have to change the subject.

Along with my grandparents, I buried a lifetime of memories filled with love, laughter, pain, and suffering. Memories of a life I have always yearned to know; memories of my heritage. My children have been fortunate. They have grown up with both sets of grandparents, enjoying all the loving gestures only grandparents can give.

Their lives have been enriched by the knowledge they have gained by seeing life through the eyes of an older person. They have learned many things they will someday pass on to their children.

Young people today are often disrespectful of the older generation. I have seen this disrespect often at the grocery store and the mall. An elderly woman struggles to open a door and a young woman pushes past her, letting the door slam in her face. For a lot of people, talking to an older person—even their own grandparents—can be difficult.

I don't blame children for their lack of compassion. I blame their parents, who perhaps feel the same way they do. Eventually—if we're lucky—we all will be part of the older generation. If you don't teach your children to have compassion and respect for their elders, you are setting yourself up for the same loneliness and isolation you put your parents through during those last years of their lives.

Empathy, tolerance, acceptance, understanding: all these qualities grow when you are around older people. Older people can make history come alive, and most of them are eager to pass things on to the younger generation so that, when they die, they're not completely dead. Having been through so many storms, the older generation can teach us all to appreciate the sunshine.

My paternal grandmother is the only one of my grandparents still alive. I'd like to share a poem I wrote about her that was published in *Sisters, The Poetry of Women*.

Abuela

Abuela is 88 years old and beautiful
With thick dark silver streaked hair,
Dressed in a flowery house dress
Sitting crookedly in her wheelchair.
Her eyes sparkle as she talks
Her soft cheeks glow,
She's happy lost in her world.

Abuela thinks she's in Cuba
In her apartment at the corner of
Almendares 120, in the city of Havana.
She offers me a *cafecito*
She'll make as soon as she's through cleaning her house
I'm not her granddaughter
I'm her cousin from Madruga
Who's gotten off the train.

I kiss her cheek and hold her fragile hand
For one brief moment she recognizes me
"*Mi nieta,*" she says smiling innocently.
Then she turns and stares into the courtyard
And slowly fades away from me.

I'm grateful for every hour and every day
Fate provides her with memories of joyous years,
Relieved she doesn't know she's far from home
Relieved she's never alone.
As I slip away quietly so as not to intrude in her special
    world,
Gnarled fingers grasp a worn-out rag
And she's cleaning her house
Waiting for Abuelo to come home from the café.

CHRISTMAS MEMORIES

The true meaning of Christmas is when deep in your heart you can hear the sound of Christmas bells ringing regardless of how small or how far away they are.

In 1963, a few months after we arrived from Cuba, I was attending Sacred Heart Catholic School in downtown McAllen. My kindergarten class was getting ready for Christmas. We hung red stockings trimmed in glitter on the bulletin board and made a beautiful manger out of cardboard.

At home, however, the only decoration we could afford was a wreath my mother had hung on the front door. During the holidays my brother and I loved to walk in downtown McAllen. We would look at all the Christmas decorations, the toys in the display windows, and make a list of all the things we wanted.

My mother would constantly remind us that someday we would be able to afford those things and much more. But this year we had to help my father save money.

On the last day of school before Christmas break, the homeroom mothers gave our class a party. On each desk, they placed a ceramic Santa cup filled with candy canes and a Christmas stocking with our names in glitter across the top.

Before we left that day, our teacher gave each of us a Christmas ornament. When I unwrapped the tissue paper, I found Pinocchio from one of my favorite stories.

Pinocchio wore green pants and a yellow shirt made of glitter. His bright red nose protruded an inch in front of his smiling face.

When I got home that day, I couldn't wait to show my mother all the things I'd received at school. My Santa cup, my stocking, and Pinocchio were the only decorations in our living room that year.

Every Christmas I bring out my Santa cup, and my mother hangs Pinocchio on her tree. Pinocchio is faded and chipped and the glitter on his shirt is practically all gone. Yet, he will always be the most important ornament on my parent's tree.

I will always treasure the memories of those first few years in the United States.

All the Christmas Eves we spent at the home of our dear friends, the Casanova's, with my husband's family and the other Cubans who had no one else in the U.S. Those Christmas Eves were filled with tears of joy and sadness. In our hearts we were all grateful to be safe in this country, but there was always the pain of being far away from our families in Cuba.

The support we gave each other during those years pulled us through very difficult times. No one had money, yet no one cared. It didn't matter who you were or what you'd had in Cuba. Here in the United States we were all in the same boat. We only had each other.

The true meaning of Christmas for me is captured in the pages of the photo albums my mother has of those years. There were pictures of my brother and me dressed in clothes my mother had made for us. There were pictures of us sitting around the table without fancy tablecloths or sterling silverware. But in those pictures, we are all smiling, hugging, dancing, and truly celebrating Christmas.

Forty years have passed since those first few Christmases, and our families have grown in numbers so that we can no longer celebrate the holidays together. The bond that was formed with these special friends has lasted a lifetime. For as long as I live, I will be grateful we had each other to share those wonderful memories together.

Reeling in a Cuban Immigrant Boy's Dream

In 1962 my husband and his family were living in a cramped apartment in Miami Beach. They had arrived from Cuba only a year before, and like most Cubans who left the country during this time, they were struggling to make a new life for themselves.

My husband was ten years old and his brother was eleven. Every week when my mother-in-law would go to the grocery store, they would wait for her in the fishing and tackle shop next door. The boys would walk around the store admiring the fishing supplies and eventually would end up in front of the fishing poles. There was nothing they wanted more than to own their own fishing pole and reel.

My mother-in-law would find her sons in the same place every week admiring the fishing poles, and it would break her heart. She knew how much the boys missed living in Cuba. They had grown up spending weekends and summers on their grandfather's ranch horseback riding, hunting, and fishing.

My father-in-law had two jobs, but every chance he got he would take his sons fishing. The pier was only six blocks away from their small apartment, and on weekends the pier would be filled with fishermen. You could tell who the Miami residents were and who the Cuban refugees were just by looking at their fishing gear. The Cubans fished with a spool of fishing wire, a hook, and a small weight tied to the end of the line.

For the Cubans fishing was fun and one of the few activities they could do with their children that was free. And if they were lucky, it could also provide dinner for their families.

My father-in-law also used fishing as an opportunity to practice his English. While they fished, he would talk to the people he met on the fishing pier. Many of them were retired Jewish businessmen who had moved to Miami Beach.

One Sunday morning they walked the six blocks to the pier. After finding an empty spot to fish, they swung the string over their heads and threw the lines out as far as they could. They fished most of the morning and, except for a few bites, no one had caught anything until my brother-in-law felt a tug on his line.

He began to reel the wire in, and as he did he could feel the fish at the other end trying to pull free. It was enormous. Slowly he continued to reel it in. By this time people on the pier had put down their fishing gear and gathered around my brother-in-law waiting to get a glimpse of the monster fish he had at the end of the line.

Just when he thought he couldn't hang on any longer, out of the water popped a fishing pole and reel covered with seaweed and mud. Everyone groaned in disappointment, except my husband and his brother who couldn't believe their eyes.

The fishing pole looked like it had been in the water for months. The reel was rusted and in bad shape, but that night my father-in-law took it apart, laid the pieces on the dining room table, and began to clean and grease every single inch.

The next weekend when the brothers went fishing, they walked to the pier carrying a fishing pole. It wasn't like the ones they had seen at the store, but for two young Cuban refugees, it was just as good.

Finding that fishing pole gave the boys hope that someday things would get better. Sometimes life has a way of pushing the clouds away and letting the sunshine through when we least expect it.

Honor the Sacrifices your Parents have Made

The other day I was watching a television show about a little boy who was ashamed to invite his father to speak to his class. His classmates' parents were doctors, lawyers, or had some kind of interesting profession. The boy's father owned a meat market-deli.

The boy loved his father, and he felt guilty about feeling this way. One afternoon he visited a family friend, and he found out that after a recent flood in the area his own father had helped feed families who had lost their homes. Not only had his father helped these families during the crisis, he was still giving one family meat every week. His father was doing all this and had never expected anything in return.

The day his father was supposed to visit his classroom, the boy stood in front of his classmates and told them how much he had hurt his father and how ashamed he was of the way he had acted.

Last week I was at the grocery store when I heard a daughter turn to her mother and say, "*Callate no hables.*" Then she turned and spoke to the cashier in English. Her mother had been trying to speak English. The older woman's face, the pain, the humiliation she felt is something no one should ever feel.

I remember in elementary school sitting next to my mom at a PTA meeting and translating to Spanish what the principal was saying. Even today, though both my parents can understand the English language, I am comfortable speaking to them only in Spanish. Their Cuban accent is something I am not ashamed of. The fact that they spoke to us in Spanish instead of just

English is something for which I am very grateful. They speak English with a Cuban accent, but I can speak, read, and write Spanish—a gift I will cherish for the rest of my life, and one I am passing on to my children.

I grew up speaking two languages, living with two different customs, and I feel this has given me twice the opportunities others have had. The more languages you know, the more people you can communicate with, the more books you can read, and the richer your life will be.

There are many families in the Rio Grande Valley whose grandparents, and maybe even their parents, don't speak English. There are families whose parents don't have a high school degree, and yet their children are teachers, lawyers, and doctors.

These parents have spent their lives working hard, barely making ends meet, yet have somehow managed to give their children the opportunity to get an education. It does not matter what your parents do. If it is honest work, you should always be proud of them. Sometimes the sacrifices of one generation can change the future of the next generation.

Your family is part of who you are. To be successful in life is to honor them and give them the place they deserve, especially if the reason you are where you are today has something to do with them.

Hang all the degrees you want on your wall, but if you are ashamed of *who* you are, you will never be a success. To be successful in life is to embrace the past, to learn from it, and to respect those who helped you along the way.

It is important to honor your heritage and the customs with which you were raised. Bring those customs into the life you are living today. Treasure your past, honor your parents, and never be ashamed of who you are.

SOURCES

[1] Thomas Blake from *Think on These Things,* Joyce Hifler, p. 3, Double Day and Company, Inc. 1966.

[2] *The Great American Bathroom Book Compact Classics,* p. 3-CA, Lan. E. England, Publisher.

[3] Christian Nestell Bovee, *The Dictionary of Thoughts, A Cyclopedia of Quotations,* p. 428, Standard Book Company, 1963.

[4] *The Great American Bathroom Book Compact Classics,* p. 3-CA, Lan C. England, Publisher.

[5] Jeremy Taylor, *The New Dictionary of Thoughts, A Cyclopedia of Quotations,* p. 666, Standard Book Company, Inc. 1966.

[6] Harry Ward Beecher, *The New Dictionary of Thoughts, A Cyclopedia of Quotations,* p. 137, Standard Book Company, 1966.

[7] Joyce Hifler, *Think on These Things,* p. 64, Doubleday and Company, Inc., 1966.

ABOUT THE AUTHOR

Maria Luisa Salcines was born in Guantánamo, Cuba and emigrated to the United States in 1963. Her work has appeared throughout the nation in newspapers, anthologies, and magazines. She is a columnist for *The Monitor* newspaper in McAllen, Texas.

She has two grown sons and lives with her husband and daughter in McAllen, Texas.

Mrs. Salcines is the Director of Redirecting Children's Behavior of the Rio Grande Valley. She is a certified parent educator for The International Network for Children and Families. She works with school districts as a consultant giving workshops and parenting classes in Redirecting Children's Behavior and Redirecting for a Cooperative Classroom. As a Parent Instructor Network Trainer (PINT), she certifies individuals interested in teaching the Redirecting Children's Behavior (RCB) course.

The RCB course teaches practical parenting skills that will help parents raise their children in a respectful, positive, and loving home. Redirecting for a Cooperative Classroom (RCC) is a dynamic course that addresses behavior management issues. The course teaches techniques that teachers will be able to use to create a peaceful and encouraging classroom environment.

As a Corporate Empowerment Consultant, Mrs. Salcines provides training in Redirecting Corporate America (RCA), which offers an alternative way of thinking that empowers and nurtures a dynamic synergy between team members. The training teaches companies, working groups, CEO's and managers skills that will build committed teams and cooperative relationships that will enrich and revitalize the work place.

For more information about workshops and courses offered in English and Spanish, visit—

www.redirectingchildrenrgv.org

or call Redirecting Children's Behavior Rio Grande Valley (956) 631-7667 or write Mrs. Salcines, 109 South 17th Street, McAllen, Texas 78501.

Mrs. Salcines is the coauthor of *Maggie's Visit to the Playroom, Play Time for Molly, Matt's in Trouble Again,* and *Matt Otra Vez en Problemas.* These children's books are on play therapy, filial therapy and school counseling. For more information about these books, visit www.marlinbooks.com.

Mrs. Salcines is a frequent guest speaker in schools and community organizations where she shares her experiences as a Cuban immigrant and a writer. For author visits and fees, contact LangMarc Publishing at email—

langmarc@booksails.com
or marialuisasalcines.com.

— TO ORDER —
Little Things Remembered

LANGMARC PUBLISHING
P.O. 90488
Austin, Texas 78709-0488

or call toll free: 1-800-864-1648
or e-mail: langmarc@booksails.com
web site: www.langmarc.com

Credit cards accepted
U.S.A. Price (English or Spanish versions) $12.95
— Texas Residents add sales tax: $1.05 —
Shipping $3 (50 cents for each additional book)

- -

Send _____ copies of English version of *Little Things
Remembered* to:

Send _____ copies of Spanish version of *Little Things
Remembered* to:

_____

_____

_____

Your phone: _____ Amt. enclosed: _____

Credit card#: _____ Expires: _____

www.ingramcontent.com/pod-product-compliance
Lightning Source LLC
Chambersburg PA
CBHW030018290326
41934CB00005B/386

9 7 8 1 8 8 0 2 9 2 7 5 4